CREATIVE PASTORAL CA

WHEN FAITH IS TESTED

Pastoral Responses to Suffering and Tragic Death

JEFFRY R. ZURHEIDE

FORTRESS PRESS   MINNEAPOLIS

WHEN FAITH IS TESTED
Pastoral Responses to Suffering and Tragic Death

Scripture quotations, unless otherwise noted, are from the Revised Standard Version Bible, copyright © 1946, 1952, 1971 by the Division of Christian Education of the National Council of the Churches of Christ. Used by permission.

Excerpts from Karl Barth, *Church Dogmatics*, ed. G. W. Bromiley and T. F. Torrance, vol. 3 © 1969, vol. 4 © 1969 T&T Clark, Edinburgh. Used by permission.

Cover design: Brad Norr/Craig Claeys
Cover art: "The Sick Child" by Edvard Munch (1863–1944), Norwegian. Used by permission of SuperStock, Inc.

Library of Congress Cataloging-in-Publication Data

Zurheide, Jeffry R., 1955–
    When faith is tested : pastoral responses to suffering and tragic death / Jeffry R. Zurheide.
        p.   cm. — (Creative pastoral care and counseling series)
    Includes bibliographical references (p.).
    ISBN 0-8006-2978-7 (alk. paper)
    1. Pastoral counseling. 2. Suffering—Religious aspects— Christianity. 3. Theodicy. I. Title. II. Series.
BV4012.2.Z87   1997
259'.6—dc21   97-21560
                                             CIP

The paper used in this publication meets the minimum requirements of American National Standards for Information Sciences—Permanence of Paper for Printed Library Materials, ANSI Z329.48.1984.

Manufactured in the U.S.A.   AF 1-2978

01   00   2   3   4   5   6   7   8   9   10

To Kristen,
who taught me much about
life, death, and pastoral care

CONTENTS

EDITOR'S FOREWORD

Perhaps no other issue confounds seminary students I work with more than the "Why did God allow this to happen" question of a parishioner. Indeed, no pastoral care situation causes me to stumble more than when I face the issue of theodicy. Tom Oden contends that it is the Gordian knot of practical theology. The author of *When Faith is Tested: Pastoral Responses to Suffering and Tragic Death*, Jeff Zurheide, about ten years ago was in a class I was teaching when it was interrupted by a message for him to call home in an emergency. He had to return home as soon as possible—ninety miles away—to be with his first-born child, who had a serious medical problem. The child died. What had been a difficult pastoral care issue for him, suffering, as it is for most of us, now became an extremely personal issue. This book is the result of his reflections, not only on his personal loss, but also the suffering and losses of the many people he has served as a hospital chaplain and as a parish pastor. He offers us insights on how to offer care to those who are not only devastated by a tragedy but also are plagued by "why" questions.

Jeffry Zurheide opens the book by discussing how we enter the lives of those who are suffering. He speaks of some of the typical mistakes that many of us make and how we can best go about listening and responding to those who are experiencing this double adversity. In chapter 2 he helps us assess what sufferers are wanting when they are asking "Why me?" Sometimes "Why did God allow this to happen to me?" is a poetic question—a way for people to say that they are in immense pain and need someone to walk the journey with them. At other times the question is, in fact, a serious theological wrestling with the gods into which the pastor is asked to enter. Zurheide helps us to diagnose the real meaning of "why" questions. In chapters 3, 4, and 5 he directly addresses the theological issue of theodicy. He uses the work of Karl Barth to make sense theologically of unmerited suffering. In chapters 6, 7, and 8 he specifically returns to pastoral care and helps the reader offer pastoral care in cases where theodicy is manifested. And finally, in chapter 9 he pleads for mystery. Theodicy's "why" questions ultimately are a mystery—and mysteries are not to be analyzed away, but approached with reverence.

It is my hope that *When Faith Is Tested* will challenge you, the reader, to look more closely at how you care for those who are suffering and how you respond to the "why" questions they ask. Zurheide in this book has given us one more chance to reflect on the issue of theodicy and he has contributed to our consideration of this mystery.

HOWARD W. STONE

INTRODUCTION

Nothing assaults a pastor's theology and emotions as does a visit to someone who is suffering and dying or who is grieving a tragic death. All of one's personal issues surrounding pain and finitude are summoned forth. All of one's presuppositions about God are challenged. Patients, their families, caregivers, and pastors struggle with such questions as, "What kind of a God could let this happen?"; "Why doesn't God heal in this situation?"; "Where is God's supposed power in this hopeless case?" These are all very human questions. They are appropriate questions. They are ancient and to some degree unanswerable questions.

This book is intended to assist clergy who are called upon to minister to the hurting and dying. And even though such a responsibility should indeed be counted a privilege (in fact, it has been for me one of the most personally rewarding and fulfilling dimensions of my own ministry), those caregivers for whom death and dying are uncharted territories can experience a great deal of anxiety when thrust into crises of these proportions.

It is important at the very outset to differentiate between various levels of suffering. If we do not, we run the risk, as J. Christiaan Beker aptly points out, of assuming that the human race is comprised of innocent victims who are not at all responsible for the ills they experience. We must distinguish tragic suffering from just suffering, just suffering from redemptive suffering, human evil from universal evil.[1] This book will focus on universal evil and suffering at the tragic level, and on how pastoral care might be expressed to those persons who have experienced the same. I will be centering my attention upon those who are victimized by suffering to which they neither contributed nor desired to some sacrificial end.

Having said this, however, it is quite impossible at this point in medical science to rule out the likelihood that in some way we all contribute to our illnesses, not to mention the illnesses of others. Whether

1

"just" suffering has only to do with willful intent is quite a complex issue. I do think, however, that it is important to make some theoretical distinctions between these levels of suffering; at the same time I believe chain-smoking cancer patients need just as much pastoral care as do those lung cancer patients who seem to have contributed very little to their demise except for breathing.

Nine chapters comprise this work. First, issues of preparation and posture are discussed. Rather than entering the room of a sufferer aggressively with a preconceived agenda in hand, it is critical that we position ourselves in such a way that we honor that person's context and adorn the pastoral self with humility.

Next we examine the question "Why me?" and offer some alternatives to this being interpreted solely on the basis of doctrine. Indeed, theology may be what a sufferer desires to discuss, but often there is something else equally significant at the heart of the matter. Chapter 3 explores common answers to the theological "Why Me?"

Chapters 4 through 6 give attention to unpacking some of the theological issues implicit in theodicy—the problem of evil—including the basis for the philosophical tensions that evil and tragic suffering produce. Karl Barth's perspectives on incarnation and omnipotence are offered as theological rationales for caregiving.

Three cases are presented in verbatim style in chapter 7 in order to apply theology to practice. The book concludes with a chapter on pastoral follow-up and another that pleas for pastoral carers to allow mystery to remain intact as we both theologize and do the work of ministry.

1

BEFORE YOU ENTER

I find it a rather sobering reality that while landscapers spend days preparing the soil for a new lawn, and painters scrape, putty, and sand wood before applying a brush, and teachers invest hours of research and reflection in each and every lecture, pastoral carers often tend to fall into their visits. Given the potential magnitude of the issues discussed during most pastoral care interactions, especially those with critically ill or bereaved persons, shouldn't such encounters receive just a bit more forethought and planning? An unqualified "yes" is the appropriate response, but how, specifically, might one prepare? Let us now examine some specifics as to how the pastoral carer might enter a caring relationship with a higher degree of intentionality.

PREPARATION

Before we even set foot into a suffering patient's room or a grieving parishioner's home it is crucial that we try to anticipate where that person might be physically, emotionally, and spiritually. Thomas Oden terms this discipline *empathy*—the "pre-condition of all therapeutic effectiveness."[1] Oden's definition is helpful: "Empathy is the process of placing oneself in the framework of another, perceiving the world as the other perceives it, sharing his or her world imaginatively."[2]

I am confident that most of us have experienced conversation (or maybe I should say parallel monologues) in which we have "missed" the other person: interactions that proved to be less than satisfactory because party "A" lacked a vital piece of information about party "B" and vice versa. When this occurs in a pastoral care setting it can be disastrous. Pastoral aloofness or distance is bad enough, but inaccurate empathy can be disconcerting at best and potentially alienating. If we are going to place ourselves truly within the framework of another, we must first discern what that framework is, both objectively and subjectively.

3

Empathy's objective dimension includes data-gathering. What is the nature of this person's illness? What is the prognosis? How has the person been handling things thus far in terms of articulation and/or affect? In my experience both as a hospital chaplain and later as a pastor, most doctors and nurses (not to mention family members) are willing to release such general information, provided there is a sufficient level of trust and mutual respect. How detailed this information is will depend upon the confidentiality policies of each particular hospital setting.

Empathy's subjective dimension is imaginative. Based upon the information gathered, how might Mr. Jones be feeling following a less than successful surgery versus a successful one? What tremendously conflicting feelings might Ms. White be experiencing following her mastectomy? What depth of disorientation and despair might Frank know after losing his wife of almost fifty years?

The one word of caution I would offer as we engage in this kind of preencounter preparation has to do with projection. Notice that I asked above, "How *might* Mr. Jones or Ms. White feel?" It is less than therapeutic to prejudge what a person *must* be feeling when that person is not you. Even if you personally have had an experience of loss very similar to the patient or parishioner for whom you are seeking to care, you cannot assume that they are going to feel, think, or react the way you did. Such presumption misses the entire point of our entering *their* frame of reference.

In addition to data gathering and extending ourselves into what we think the sufferer's framework might be, prayer is an essential spiritual preparation. If our goal is indeed to empathize, should we not seek to align ourselves with the One who empathized in an ultimate way with our world? "The Word (who was with God and is God) became flesh and dwelt among us, full of grace and truth" (John 1:14) is not merely a pleasant Advent text but a theological affirmation linking God intimately with this world. Again, we turn to Oden:

> Incarnation means that God assumes our frame of reference, entering into our human situation of finitude and estrangement, sharing our human condition even unto death.[3]

The shortest verse in the Bible is probably one of the most significant in this regard: "Jesus wept" (John 11:35). If we take seriously the notion that God was incarnate in the Word, Jesus Christ, then the image of a weeping God becomes all the more powerful. What a symbol of empathy! God shed tears on behalf of the world God entered, and continues to shed tears for those who suffer. As Paul admonishes us to "weep with those who weep" (Rom. 12:15), so suffering hospital patients might also be reminded that *God* weeps with those who weep, and that God weeps when *they* weep. "Jesus wept" must always be read as "Jesus weeps." This empathy of God's must be seen as an active empathy, an empathy that is also extended and augmented by us, God's people.

In this sense, the notion of incarnation travels full circle. God became incarnate in Jesus Christ, but those seeking to follow in Jesus' footsteps must in turn seek to incarnate him. Carlyle Marney picks up on this when he states:

> The content of our drama is that it happened once. This is the basis for our preachment. Incarnation as the answer to the matter-spirit risk was acted out. And the word . . . was made flesh . . . and grace . . . ministered to faith . . . in such a way that person . . . will act as though he were an incarnation too.[4]

We've most likely heard the story before. Nightmares awakened a young boy in the middle of the night. He cried out for his mother who quickly joined him at bedside. He said, "I'm afraid, Mommy." She hugged him and assured him that he need not be afraid, for not only was she going to be sleeping one room away, but God was right by his side also. "Well I know God's here," insisted the boy, "but tonight I guess I just needed somebody with skin on."

God's empathic presence can be known to the sufferer through us, the "somebodies with skin on." We love because God first loved us (1 John 4:19), we weep because God first wept for us, we care because One cared for us to such an extent that God shared our human condition even unto death.

Through data gathering, extending ourselves imaginatively into what the other person's framework might be, and aligning ourselves with God through Jesus Christ in previsit prayer, our pastoral care sessions will take on a greater degree of intentionality and increase the likelihood that an empathic, person-to-person connection will be made.

POSTURE

It is at this point that we consider the question of posture when visiting the suffering. As persons seeking to minister we must be clear in our minds as to who we are, who we are not, and what we truly have to offer.

In my experience as a chaplain, I often had the opportunity to play the role of a kind of pastoral spectator as clergy would come in from the community to offer care. Many offered empathic and appropriate support. But there were others whose styles might be classified under the headings of "Guru," "Doctor," and "Sunbeam."

Guru

It is such a temptation for pastoral carers to become walking "treasuries of wisdom" for the suffering. The hook might find its barb in the fact that clergy who have attended four years of college plus three years of seminary and perhaps even more clinical training or graduate work beyond that are placed in a kind of Solomonic role, a role that conjures up the expectation from within (self) and from without (parishioners and others) that the pastoral carer should be able both to address and to fix suffering with scriptural or theological answers.

"Tell me why this is happening to me, Pastor."

"With all of your theological training share with me how I can pray and be healed, Father."

"Give me the scriptural formula that will unlock this mystery for me, Chaplain."

Such pleadings can be very seductive, causing some pastoral carers seriously to compromise their own theologies in order to tell suffering people what they seem to want to hear.

Add to these expectations the dynamics of the typical hospital setting and the heat is really on. Just think about the scenario. Doctors offer treatment, the nursing staff offers medication and a regimen of care, social workers offer placement and financial counseling, the support staff offers testing, transporation, T.V., and meals. Why, even the custodial staff contributes by cleaning and disinfecting the rooms with mop and sponge in hand. And so the question then becomes, "What do you have to offer, Pastor? What objective help can you provide?"

So what's a pastoral carer to do in the face of such internal and external pressure? Some become gurus who dispense answers (albeit deficient or even pathological ones) to those they visit. The kinds of answers that are typically given are chronicled in a later section of this book, but suffice it to say at this point that pastoral carers are not gurus, nor should they feel pressured into trying to fulfill such an inappropriate role. Rather, we seek to bring the presence and empathizing love of God, along with counsel and the resources of faith (Scripture, prayer, sacraments), to suffering people. That is what we have to offer. If it seems too little then we may need to reexamine our own internal issues related to pastoral role, calling, and identity. Remembering who we are and what we have to offer, and then proceeding to put some mental fences around what we conclude, will contribute greatly to a sense of security and confidence as we do the work of ministering to the hurting.

Doctor

It is an additional temptation for the pastoral carer to play the role of medical doctor when making hospital calls. This role has the clergyperson discussing tests, procedures, and diagnoses he or she knows little about except for some personal experience with a similar surgery or an account in a news magazine or hearsay. Now in an environment steeped in medical technology and terminology it is somewhat understandable that one feel constrained to keep pace with it all. But again, it comes back to the issue of identity. Pastoral carers are not expected to be knowledgeable of medical science. That is not our discipline. We have other issues to discuss.

Clinical psychologist Paul Pruyser chides ministers because of our tendency to avoid the very issues most parishioners expect us to address—that is, to explore what is happening to them and support them using theological terms and images.[5] Who else is going to approach their crisis with such a perspective? What other professional is going to feel sufficiently competent to help them interpret their existential crisis from a biblical or theological point of view? The answer is no one.

"No, Mr. Brown, I don't know why they still have you on that medication. However, I do sense your fear. Tell me where you are in all of this."

"I don't know much about bypass surgery, Mrs. Winter, but tell me how you're feeling about going in tomorrow."

Pastoral carers occupy a unique place on the support team. No, we are not doctors, and most of our parishioners do not necessarily want to make doctors of us. In the words of my junior high soccer coach, "Play your position!" If we could only do precisely that, and play our "pastoral positions," all would stand to benefit—sufferers and carers alike.

Sunbeam

Some pastors and chaplains go about their visitation under the banner, "Jesus wants me for a sunbeam." It is a delightful chorus, but a less than adequate model for doing pastoral care. The thesis seems to be that a happy person is a whole person, and that if a sufferer can somehow be "cheered up" there is great utility and virtue therein.

I have several problems with this thesis. First, such a theology of "happy elation" does not square with the experience of Jesus himself, not to mention the wider thrust of Scripture. Jesus warned, "In the world you have tribulation, but be of good cheer, I have overcome the world" (John 16:33). Yes, there is ultimate victory inherent in this passage, but notice that the victory is through the great Overcomer himself. And in this great overcoming Jesus suffered, bled, and died. In the midst of his passion there was little visible joy but plenty of anxiety, struggle, and agony. We see nothing of a sunbeam trudging up Golgotha's hill.

A similar dynamic is evident in the life of Paul, who in the midst of his apostolic triumphs also experienced the nagging vulnerability of "the thorn in the flesh" (2 Cor. 12:7). Here too we see a kind of veiled victory at best—"My grace is sufficient for you." This was God's only response to Paul's fervent prayer that the thorn be removed. Comforted he may have been, but sunbeam he was not.

It has been said by another that "when we close the door on reality it breaks in a window." How very true! Adopting a "hail fellow well met"[6] pastoral care posture that is all grins serves to close the door on a suffering person's realities. It does not square with their frame of reference, nor does it connect with where they most likely are. And the tragedy is that after a sunbeam-style pastor or chaplain leaves the room, reality can indeed break in the window with few around ready and able to pick up the pieces.

A second area of concern regarding this sunbeam posture has to do with the key to all therapeutic effectiveness—empathy. I have discovered that it is a rather widespread assumption among family members, medical staff, patients, and parishioners alike that the true mark of a successful pastoral care interaction is to "leave 'em smiling." But does not this assumption trivialize spirituality, while also doing an injustice to the sufferer's context? Might it not be the case, at times, that accurate pastoral empathy will leave a patient in tears? Is it not possible that putting a parishioner in touch with their reality will serve to induce grief rather than frivolity? There will be times when tears—not smiles—will indeed be the mark of a successful pastoral care interaction. The reminder "God's grace is sufficient for you" in the face of great suffering will most likely not produce effervescence but a quiet, reflective assurance that transcends smiles. Accurate empathizers, yes—sunbeams, no.

THE ENTRANCE

After one has adequately prepared for a pastoral visit and has anticipated his or her pastoral posture, the entrance itself becomes the next crucial issue. How is one to enter the sufferer's home or hospital room? Humbly and openly, with a generous helping of silence.

Pastoral Humility

Entering the domain of a sufferer might be compared with our entering a sanctuary—a holy place. Inasmuch as parents tend to hush their children engaged in raucous behavior in a place designated for worship, pastoral carers might similarly clothe themselves with reverence. Accurate empathy demands such a stance. And common sense informs us that both the persons in pain and the spaces wherein that pain is experienced deserve better than a flippant, casual treatment.

As a hospital chaplain, I was regularly called upon to visit persons whom I did not know, which necessitated an entrance that was characteristically measured and cautious. This will not be the case for those of us who primarily visit our own parishioners. A sense of rapport in that situation can only help; but lest familiarity breed contempt, even those whom we might deem intimates are entitled to a hearty dose of respect and sensitivity. Consider their present context, as well as the transitional trauma of it all. Imagine that many of the patients we visit felt carefree, happy, and whole yesterday. Suddenly they feel anything but! Privacy is a thing of the past. Freedom is no more. It may even appear that the medical staff will decide their fate (technicians subjecting them to unpleasant if not painful tests, nurses determining when they will sleep, brush their teeth, be needled and prodded). Their new context is also one of extreme vulnerability. Worry and grief have a way of wearing persons down, debilitating the entire personality, sapping the vitality of sufferers. Pain takes a significant toll on the human beings it visits.

In light of these contextual considerations, it seems only appropriate that pastoral carers enter the spaces of the suffering with a sense of humility, even privilege. For we are about to enter a sanctuary that is not ours to fathom or control, but only to share. If there is any time to treat a person as "thou"—to borrow Martin Buber's classic designation[7]—it is now, when that person comes face to face with the ultimate questions and struggles of life. Be humbled by such pain. Bow your spirit as you enter.

Pastoral Openness

Some pastors tend to bombard their parishioners with questions, comments, even theological recitations, but this is hardly the way to initiate an empathizing bond. Rather than immediately launching out with a preconceived agenda for the visit, it is preferable that the pastoral carer allow the patient to take the lead. Entering the framework of another demands that we sit back and let the other set the pace. As the conversation unfolds the one for whom we are seeking to care will reveal to us what is going on and what he or she wants to discuss, determining how the visit will eventuate.

"Leading the witness," one of the more frequent "objections" on the part of T.V. courtroom lawyers, is likewise often encountered by sufferers. Don't we all find it rather objectionable, even under the best of circumstances, either to be led in conversation by another or to have our verbal pauses filled in whenever we might hesitate to locate the appropriate word? Now of course the assumption on the other person's part is that they know exactly what we're going through. (We've already determined, above, that that is a dangerous assumption for pastoral carers.) And so the sufferer, our witness, is all too often led through the visit as if he or she were a child. (And even with children this is not especially appropriate!)

Sufferers tend to supply pastoral carers with initial cues—visible and audible data about what they're experiencing on that particular day, during that particular hour. Notice these cues.

What do you see in the patient's eyes: pain, fatigue, relief? What sort of a mood does her countenance project: contentment, apathy, irritability? How about the tone of the voice? Does this person struggle to speak? Does his or her greeting seem affected or forced? What about body language?—perhaps the parishioner doesn't establish eye contact, or slumps in the chair, or is favoring a particular limb or surgical site.

All of these cues, if we are attentive to them, enable us to practice pastoral openness. So, in essence, what we are doing is allowing the parishioner to give us a sense (albeit inconclusive) as to whether or not the visit is well-timed, what might be going on within the person, and how he or she might want to make use of the visit.

Sometimes I have found it helpful to almost immediately mirror back (Rogerian style) what I sense about the person, especially if the data is compelling. I might remark, "Mary, it looks like you're in a lot of pain," or "It looks like you're having a rough day, John," or (when the person seems withdrawn) "Is this a good time for me to visit or would it be better for me to stop by again tomorrow?" This is the sufferer's opportunity to take the lead. If I inaccurately processed something she can then indicate, "No, this is an OK time to visit; it's just that this back pain is getting to me," or "Please sit with me for a while; I'm glad you came."

After a brief silence the pastoral carer might ask open-ended questions such as, "Tell me how it's going" or "What's been happening to you the last couple of days?" A measured cluster of such open-ended queries serves to draw out the person. What you're seeking is personal, even visceral, data as to how that individual is faring. Asking only closed, "yes–no" questions is more akin to the game "Twenty Questions" than to empathic ministry. Remarks such as "It's really tough to be in the hospital during this season, isn't it?" or "It must be scary to be facing such extensive surgery" only project our own fears onto the other person, supplying our captive audience with feelings and issues initiated by us!

If accurate empathy is truly our aim, an open, nondirective approach is essential. The key here, for the pastoral carer, is to engender within oneself an ability to be led.

Silence

It is the tendency of most of us human beings to fill silence with nervous chatter. This is the case around a dinner table or in the context of a support group, and it seems to be especially rampant in hospital rooms.

Frederick Buechner, in his book *Telling the Truth*, describes the way in which the bound, beaten Christ holds silence out "like a terrible gift" to the beleaguered Pilate.[8] When the latter asks, "What is truth?" Jesus allows the silence itself to descend and beckon.

Silence can indeed be terrible for those of us who have reason to feel its threat. Yet it can also be seen as "gift" when it draws forth from the human heart such realities as guilt, pain, grief, or joy.

It has often been the case for me in the counseling context that the silence that follows a particularly poignant disclosure elicits profound emotions. Counselees will ponder, gasp out loud, or cry as they grasp for the first time some truth about themselves, as silence has been allowed to unfold. Even so, it remains such a temptation to fill the silence with words. The parishioners and patients we visit will be tempted to do so, and the uninitiated pastoral carer will do the same.

Walter Wangerin tells of the time he first learned about the significance of pastoral silence:

> In the second year of my ministry at Grace, Joselyn Fields fell sick.
>
> In the spring they diagnosed a cancer. In summer they discovered that it had metastasized dramatically. By autumn she was dying. She was forty-seven years old.
>
> Spring, summer, and autumn, I visited the woman.
>
> For most of that time I was a fool and right fearful to sit beside her; but I visited the woman.
>
> Well, I didn't know what to say, nor did I understand what I had the right to say. I wore out the Psalms; Psalms were safe. I prayed often that the Lord's will be done, scared to tell either him or Joselyn what the Lord's will ought to be, and scared of his will anyway. I bumbled.
>
> One day when she awoke from surgery, I determined to be cheerful, to enliven her and to avoid the spectre that unsettled me—the death. I chattered. I spoke brightly of the sunlight outside, and vigorously of the tennis I had played that morning, sweetly of the flowers, hopefully of the day when she would sit again at the organ, reading music during my sermon—
>
> But Joselyn rolled a black eye my way. She raised one bony finger to my face. And she said, "Shut up."

God help me!—I learned so slowly. But God in Joselyn taught me with an unutterable patience. I, who had thought to give her the world she did not have, was in fact taking away the only world she did have. I had been canceling her serious, noble, faithful and dignified dance with death.

I shut up. I learned. I kept visiting her. I earned my citizenship.[9]

We earn our citizenship when we learn that silence during a pastoral visit is not only okay but highly appropriate. For in our silence, are we not incarnating the presence of God who is also silent? Since we do not have all the answers nor the magic words to make everything "right," is not silence a gift to be cherished, representing, as it were, the beckoning power of God?

A terse "shut up" is perhaps what most of us pastoral carers need to hear as we rush to fill the lingering silence with verbage. We need not fear silence. Rather we ought to reverence it, viewing it as the very conduit through which the grace and presence of God can be known.

2

ASSESSING WHAT SUFFERERS SEEK

Even after good preparation, appropriate posture, and a therapeutic entrance have been achieved, many pastoral carers seem to goad the interaction toward theology. It is such a temptation for clergy to move too quickly to attempt a theological "answer" when a theological question has not necessarily been posed. There are most likely several reasons for this propensity. It may be the realm where we feel the most comfortable. It is cerebral, objective, and a ready refuge for clergy who want to get close, but not *too* close, to the pain of others. After all, isn't theology the very medicine we have been trained and called to dispense? Theology certainly occupies a crucial place in the scheme of things, but genuine empathy—entering the framework of another—calls upon us to hear what the person is truly needing and requesting at that point and time. Determining at the outset how the pastoral interaction should proceed is the art upon which this chapter will focus.

THE RHETORICAL "WHY ME?"

When a hospitalized patient or a bereaved spouse grieving at home asks, "Why is this happening to me?" it is important that the pastoral carer take a "Selah" moment; that is, a ten-second time out to pause.[1] Does every "Why me?" necessarily beg for a treatise on theodicy and its impact on the doctrine of providence? I think not. The impassioned question "Why me?" can also be rhetorical—a question that does not expect an answer.

The scenario is this: Malcolm and Sue have just lost their infant daughter of six months to a genetic anomaly that was known to be terminal. The child died while you, the pastor, were out of town and you came to the house as soon as you returned that evening. After the initial subdued greeting at the door, the three of you move to the living room and begin the conversation. You open with, "Tell me about what happened to Kathy." Malcolm starts by walking you through the times and details, but Sue interrupts, sobbing, "Why? Why did God do this to us? We were just getting to know her and then she is snatched from us. Why? Why?"

Several possible responses present themselves. You could highlight Sue's apparent hysteria and suggest that she seek the care of a physician. (If you choose this option, you should expect the conversation either to become very heated or to come to a grinding halt.) Alternatively, you could launch into a Bible study, if you indeed sensed during your ten-second Selah that a theological question was being asked here. Or could it be that what Sue is really doing is venting her grief and allowing her question to serve as a kind of emotional catharsis?

Sometimes the last thing mourners want or need is answers, even though they may indeed be speaking in the interrogative. Perhaps what Sue is wanting most of all is to be heard; to be given the opportunity to express her excruciating outrage to another human being, or to God, or to the individual who comes into her home representing God. Sit; be silent; listen to the cries of a woman perhaps more capable of expressing her feelings than Malcolm, who verbally and physically tries to stifle their grief with: "There now, it's going to be OK."

Whenever I have witnessed well-meaning carers or mourners themselves trying to keep the lid on grief, I have often gently contradicted them with, "No, tears are important; you need to grieve"; or, "This is an incredible loss. Crying is indeed appropriate." It is far too often the case that mourners need permission to express their grief, to do what feels natural and cathartic.

The best way to discourage healthy grieving[2] is for pastoral carers to answer what may be a rhetorical question—"Why me?"—with sermons. That will stymie the vulnerability of tears more effectively than anything.

There is a direct way to check whether Sue is asking "Why me?" in a rhetorical sense. Following a good long Selah pause and an interval of attentive listening, the pastoral carer might offer something like, "I hear your pain, Sue, but help me; do you want me to respond, or just hear you out?" Such a "rhetorical check" invites the hurting individual to state rather explicitly how they would like to use the visit. If we are to be truly "there" for them, such guidance is invaluable in helping us to determine our approach. Hopefully Sue would then respond with, "I guess I just need to talk for a while"; or "No, I really do want to know what you think, Pastor." With that bit of data we can then move on in a more informed, intentional direction.

THE COMPANIONSHIP "WHY ME?"

Sometimes what sufferers feel they need most is to find a companion amidst their grief. Pain is intrinsically alienating. It tends to make us feel like strangers to others (even family), strangers to ourselves (in terms of confusion), and sometimes it can even make God seem like a stranger, as this One upon whom we have relied through the years may now feel distant or somehow disconnected.

In light of such alienation, pastoral carers do the sufferer a great service by offering companionship—a ministry of presence. Let's suppose that you, a hospital staff chaplain, are asked by a nurse on the critical care unit to visit with a lonely young man named Rob. Rob is experiencing the ravaging effects of AIDS, and you are told that he probably will not survive his present pneumonia. Your research indicates that he did not register any religious preference upon admission, nor does he seem to receive many visitors. And as is often the case, even the members of Rob's family are pretty much keeping their distance.

As you enter Rob's room you notice that he is pale, experiencing labored breathing through an oxygen mask, and staring out the window. Even though your entrance is quiet and respectful, Rob startles. You identify who you are and ask if it's OK for you to spend a few minutes with him. He seems to appreciate your presence and pulls the mask down a bit so that he can speak. He asks you about your denominational affiliation, and following some small talk becomes very reflective. After a silence he looks up at you and asks, "Why? Why this?" (He casts his gaze toward the window again and seems to look into the distance.) "I just wonder why." (He then grows silent and fills with tears.)

For this initial visit, since this is your first contact with Rob, it is important that some kind of a connection be made. Citizenship (per Wangerin) must be earned through silence and respect. And even though Rob asks "Why?" your Selah moment provided you the sneaking suspicion that companionship, not theological "answers," is what

Rob truly desires. Your presence, by virtue of your role as chaplain, represents God's presence in one way or another. But for one who may not be at all religious, your human presence represents human companionship, which is itself highly significant.

The Apostle Paul understood the potency of human relationship in ministry. He passionately states to the Thessalonians: "So being affectionately desirous of you we were ready to share with you not only the Gospel of God but also our own selves, because you had become very dear to us" (1 Thess. 2:8). Yes, clergy have gospel to offer, but just as importantly, according to Paul, we also offer our own selves as a healing resource. It is this dynamic of relationship which can create access to persons' ears and minds and hearts. Without it we easily become "noisy gongs and clanging cymbals."

Again, after a period of silence, a pastoral carer might employ the "companionship check" with Rob. One might ask, "I sense your pain, Rob, but help me. Are you truly asking a question or are you requesting that someone share your pain?" Perhaps he might say nothing, or respond, "I dunno." At this point I might ask amidst the silence: "Well, Rob, is it OK if I sit with you? We don't have to talk. I just want to be with you for a while."

Sometimes the companionship we offer by merely joining Rob in his pain is in itself very meaningful, if not healing. He might break the silence himself with a comment or two guiding you as to how you might proceed, or you both might sit together for ten minutes with nary a word. However little you might think you've accomplished during such a nonverbal visit, at the very least it is likely that you have earned the right to return. Moving slowly is the name of the game when doing "cold calling" on persons you have never met. We can only hope to be given the opportunity to build upon a positive, empathic beginning.

THE THEOLOGICAL "WHY ME?"

There will be instances wherein "Why me?" will genuinely be a theological question in search of an answer. Even after this becomes apparent, however, the pastoral carer still needs to sort out whether this is what the person really needs. Theology can be a cover-up not only for the visiting clergyperson but also for the patient. Theoretical discussions can keep genuine issues of fear, pain, and grief at bay even if the content might seem appropriate. I am always somewhat suspicious that I am being duped to fill the room with diversionary dogma when the individual seems to move the conversation to theology too quickly. In order to fulfill the person's wish respectfully I may briefly address a doctrinal point but then turn it around to focus upon some facet of here-and-now experience.

"What do you believe about the Holy Spirit, Pastor?" asks Helen hastily, as you barely enter the room and engage. (She is a parishioner of six years who has just been diagnosed with advanced liver cancer.) "Well, Helen, as I read the New Testament, the Holy Spirit is described as the Comforter and the one who would take Jesus' place in being with us always. It sounds to me like you could use some of the Spirit's presence and comfort in this place. Tell me about what you've heard regarding your test results."

At that point, I have honored Helen's request, but have also given her the opportunity to speak about that which I discern she really needs for us to discuss—the shocking news of her cancer. Now, even after I have sought to move the conversation in what I have concluded would be a more therapeutic (though difficult) direction, she may not be able to go there with me.

Let's say that Helen is willing to be steered toward that most painful of subjects and asks the classic, "Why me? Why did this happen to me, Pastor, when my kids need me, my husband needs me?" After some silence is allowed to unfold, one might use a "theological answer check" such as: "I don't know, and I don't pretend to have all of the answers, but if you really want to talk about where God is in all of this, I'll give it a try. Is this what you want?" If Helen answers in the affirmative, then unto theology you must go, though move carefully. As the following chapters illustrate, potential pitfalls abound.

3

ANSWERS TO THE THEOLOGICAL "WHY ME?"

Once a pastoral carer has concluded that a theological discussion is both called for by the sufferer and appropriate, one must be prepared to tread on hallowed, mysterious ground. Two formidable constraints loom large: the *time* to do the subject justice, and the *ability* to do the subject justice. Full-length sermons or lectures are not called for in light of the sufferer's limited tolerance, and even if you could run on and on into the night, you would never formulate an adequate "answer" for it all.

Sometimes the one we seek to comfort will assist us by filling in the "Why me?" blank. For instance, you might learn early in the interaction that Tom is convinced that his diabetes is the direct result of God's judgment upon him, thus providing a fairly specific ultimate issue to address. This is a good way to proceed, as it not only allows the sufferer to set the pace but also serves to narrow the scope of your response.

It is important to note at the outset that each of the following commonly suggested answers to the theological "Why me?" has at least some basis in Scripture. In fact, if thrust into a debate team competition, I think I could make a fairly good biblical case for any of them. That being said, however, each of the following interpretations can be pushed to a sadistic extreme. The burden then falls on the pastoral carer to discern whether the interpretation to which a parishioner or patient is clinging is indeed life-giving and therapeutic or destructive. If our purpose in visiting is truly to serve our parishioners, then undoubtedly there will be times when it is necessary for us both to diagnose and to treat "sick religion." This will need to be done carefully, with a great deal of finesse, but the bottom line is that pastoral carers are called to be prophets as well as priests. A prophetic word can have great power in its effects.

THE DETERMINISTIC ANSWER

Those who come from traditions in which the "Sovereignty of God" (Calvin) is given a preeminent place in the theological pantheon will tend to seek shelter in the deterministic answer: "It's God's will." But the degree of shelter that this option affords will vary from person to person. Some sufferers will be content to allow "It's God's will" to suffice, even though by comparison with the other possible conclusions it is the most vague and mysterious.

Elsie, a sixty-eight-year-old parishioner who has just broken her hip in a major fall, finds a great deal of solace in "It's God's will." Though others scratch their heads and move on to the question that this option seems to beg—"But *why* is this God's will?"—Elsie is satisfied that a divine plan is in place, even though she understands that she will never grasp it. In your conversations with her she displays a "father knows best" understanding of God, a perspective that she believes to be consistent with the main thrust of the Bible and one with which she is personally satisfied.

We must be careful not to wrest such a notion from the hands of sufferers like Elsie just because it has been weighed and found wanting in our own minds. Yes, saying that it was God's will for her to break her hip and experience the incapacitation that such an injury will no doubt involve does reflect rather poorly upon God (as if God derives some sadistic glee from pain inflicted upon us). And no, Elsie's appreciation for the sovereignty of God doesn't necessarily have to go the way of a strict determinism (as if everything that happens in this world must be God's will if God is truly sovereign). But these are not issues for Elsie and one needs to question very seriously whether they *should* become her issues.

When I have sensed that a patient's use of the deterministic answer is indeed causing more harm than good, I have rather quizzically remarked, "I wonder what kind of God would cause a person to break her hip." Sometimes the response has been, "Oh, God didn't cause this to happen," thus opening the way for a discussion about the things that just happen in a sick world versus God *causing* all of these things to happen. Whatever tack you decide to take, just know that the deterministic answer is one with which you will undoubtedly be confronted as sufferers try to make sense of it all.

THE DIDACTIC ANSWER

This option gives a pedagogical interpretation to suffering: "God is teaching me something." Implicit in this didactic answer, however, is the all-too-often frustrating question: "But *what* is God teaching me?"

I think it's safe to say that all of life itself is a kind of "lab" experience. Everything, everywhere, at any time has teaching potential, and pain and suffering are no exception. C. S. Lewis stated at one point that God "shouts at us through our pain." Perhaps this is true. As I look back at my own life, the painful seasons were indeed poignant seasons, chapters in which I felt a heightened sense of awareness and introspection and grace. But does pain itself necessarily possess a didactic quality? Is the point of all pain learning, or is learning more of a natural by-product of the experience of pain? Mr. Ling feels that there is a lesson for him in his bout with leukemia. When you, as chaplain, ask, "What do you sense God is teaching you, Mr. Ling?" he responds that he doesn't know yet but that he is praying for wisdom. This is often the plight of those who embrace this answer. Faith for them can be reduced to a torturous game in which they feel constrained to guess what God intends the lesson to be. When I have felt the need to try to ease a person away from such an extreme, I have asked, "What kind of a God would choose a brain tumor as a learning device?" or "Do you really think God would bestow cancer upon your child in order to teach you something?"

I have heard the story told that a well-meaning friend went to visit another who had only recently undergone back surgery. Although he was still in a great deal of pain, the patient received this visitor with as much cordiality as he could muster. After an exchange of some small talk the visitor inhaled, stood tall, and asked, "So, what is God teaching you through this experience?" The patient hesitated for a moment and answered rather coolly, "God is teaching me that back surgery hurts like hell."

If God assigns pain for its lesson value, then the burden should also be placed upon God to reinforce the experience by writing the point across the blackboard. If pain is not assigned but simply and cruelly happens in a sick world, then we might choose to derive something didactic from it or choose not to. Pain comes to us with few requirements.

THE ATHLETIC ANSWER

A related view is shared by those who see personal suffering as a training or testing experience from God. When asked to substantiate this perspective, they usually appeal to the quintessential sufferer himself, Job, whose tragic losses were indeed framed as a kind of cosmic test. The problem with utilizing such an ancient and inherently mysterious story as a rationale for all suffering is that it was never intended to be used as such, nor should we take the experience of one and establish it as a kind of template for all.

Job's story does make several important points. First, the submissions of Eliphaz, Bildad, and Zophar as to the "whys" of Job's suffering were found to be inadequate from the perspective of the Almighty. (Note that theirs was the Disciplinarian Answer.) Second, what becomes apparent at the end of the story is that suffering is a mystery, the answers to which are contained in the creative authority of God; hence, "Where were you when I laid the foundation of the earth?" (Job 38:4). Attempts to substantiate the claim that all suffering is testing, based upon Job, not only miss the point of his story but may serve to trivialize suffering by giving it a hollow, athletic spin.

Seth Green has lost his job of twenty years along with medical insurance that has heretofore covered his wife Mildred's costly dialysis treatments, by means of which she is being kept alive. As you visit the home you find a Seth who is optimistic and hopeful but doing little in the way of a constructive job search. When you ask him if he feels that God is involved in his life right now or somewhat removed, he responds, "Well, the way I see it, this is sort of a test from God. He's trying to see what I am made of. He's going to see how many hits and tackles I can take."

The primary problem with the athletic view of suffering is that it distances the coach from the athlete; the trainer from the trainee; God from the sufferer. We tend to want to pass tests alone, especially if we've grown up in a culture that is steeped in approval contingent upon performance. We have come to believe that we must individually achieve, make the grade, take the hit. So it is with our view of a God who tests through suffering. We all want to become solo acts who prove, much aside from any mediating grace, that we can rise above and be more than conquerors.

A related problem with this model again has to do with how it reflects upon God. Did God single out Seth Green and decide that now is the time for him to graduate from running the spiritual 440 to the 880 by causing him to lose his job? And how about Mildred? Will the possibility that she will be prevented from receiving her much-needed dialysis treatments be worth his training?

As with the didactic answer, I think it's safe to say, that all of life can be seen as a test. Every challenge, every resistance, every thorny problem has the potential of propelling us into higher altitudes of understanding, competence, and maturity. But is every buffeting experience an assignment from God, or is it merely part and parcel of our living in a world in which all is not sweetness and light? Is every experience of suffering a scrimmage out of the celestial coach's practice book, or is it basically pain which we certainly *must* endure and from which we *might* grow?

Perhaps you, the visiting pastor, might ask such questions of the Greens, seeking to sound out their true feelings on these issues, to the end that God would become to them more of a companion in their struggles than a hard-driving coach.

THE DISCIPLINARIAN ANSWER

This option views God as the divine disciplinarian who uses pain and suffering to punish people for wrongs and sins committed. The only subtle payoff I can glean from such a view is that the one being disciplined at least has a sense that the Parent has enough interest in the child to mete out the discipline. The negatives of this option include a rather ghoulish perspective of God and the attending vexing question, "What did I do to deserve this?"

I have personally found the disciplinarian answer to be one of the more destructive options that sufferers will embrace. For it not only alienates the one chastised from God and others (the person can feel "unclean" and "untouchable"), but it is fueled by guilt. Grace gets pitched to the side and one begins to take an obsessive, sometimes sleepless, moral inventory of past sins.

Alice Stine, a forty-five-year-old ovarian cancer patient, fills in the blank of "Why is this happening to me?" with the disciplinarian answer, "Because of what I did when I was a university senior twenty-five years ago." Upon visiting her in the hospital, you, her minister, sense that she is haunted by something in her past, but hesitate to probe too deeply because of her resistance. You make a mental note of it and decide to put the subject off until the second or third visit. Two days later you visit again and say in the course of the conversation, "Alice, it may be me, but I sense that there is some distance between us. We don't know each other all that well, but is there something about God that's weighing heavily upon you? I got a glimmer of it when you asked me not to close in prayer at the end of our last visit." Alice squirms a bit and announces forthrightly, "I know why I'm going through all of this." "You mean this illness?" you ask. "Yes," she says, "God's getting even with me for something I did a long time ago."

Now let me interject at this point that sometimes those who choose this disciplinarian interpretation will have no idea what they have done to deserve such punishment. When someone makes a general statement like, "I have cancer because God is disciplining me," I will usually ask what they have done to require such a harsh sentence. I might very seriously remark, "You've been so sick with this, Alice. What have you done to deserve such suffering?" Sometimes they will come up with nothing, indicating that their sense of guilt, at least as it bears upon their illness, is not rational. Other times persons like Alice will unearth an experience which they deem "major sin."

As it turned out, Alice had an affair with a married man when she was a senior at the university. She thinks she dealt with it adequately back then, but now she is haunted by the experience, suspecting that it may be the cause of her illness. After a discussion about the biblical understanding of God's forgiveness ("As far as the East is from the West . . . ," Psalm 103:12; "If we confess . . . God will forgive . . . ," 1 John 1:9), one might proceed to address the issue of "suffering as discipline" or save that for another visit.

It is important to pace oneself and be content with one experience of illumination and consolation at a time. Alice has been reassured concerning forgiveness. That much confirmed in an intentional closing prayer (if she's willing this time) may be enough. On the next visit you might choose to explore the notion (which is held by some) that all of the world's suffering is the result of God's punishing wrath. Alice will most likely balk at that one, perhaps even identifying the hundreds of thousands of innocents around our globe, especially children, who are touched by suffering. Such a realization might help her to move away from correlating personal sin with suffering and to find a bit of grace for herself as someone to whom cancer just happened rather than as someone by whom it was deserved.

The disciplinarian answer offers pastoral carers the opportunity of opportunities to do prophetic pastoral care—leading the ones to whom we seek to minister in a genuine and holistic manner away from a destructive religious understanding to a redemptive and life-giving faith.

4

THEODICY:
THE PROBLEM OF EVIL

Technically the term *theodicy*, which is comprised of a combination of Greek and Latin terms meaning "God" and "Right," has to do with the righteousness of God in the face of human suffering. In other words, How can a good and righteous God permit evil and suffering? While this is the technical meaning of the term, there is inherent in theodicy an additional dimension: namely, the omnipotence or power of God. The corresponding and related hypothetical question would then be, Why did such a powerful God allow this suffering to occur?

A TENSION-FILLED TRIAD

The historical tensions surrounding the issue of theodicy can be summarized in the following restatement of a portion of a familiar table grace:

God is great;
God is good;

But instead of "Now we thank Him for our food," we insert, "Evil is real."[1]

"God is great" is a simplified expression of the omnipotence of God. "God is good" speaks of God's righteousness. In a pre-fallen, "Eden-like" world no other postulates would be necessary in describing reality. But in the world as we know it, we must in some way recognize another dimension, an alien factor, which is characterized by tragic suffering—universal evil. Add this reality to the omnipotence and righteousness of God and we have the great paradox of theodicy—evil existing simultaneously with a God of limitless power and goodness.

God is great; God is good; evil is real. Each of these postulates has its basis in Scripture, theology, and experience. The Bible certainly

26

affirms the truth of this troublesome triad. Personalities like Job, whose struggles with this issue were brought very close to home; David, who agonized in the Psalms over the presence of God amidst the evils that he experienced; and Paul, who sought to harmonize the God he thought he knew with his own sufferings—these are all witnesses to the formidable nature of this issue.[2] In addition, theologians from Augustine to Luther, Leibniz to Barth, have addressed the problems inherent in this triad of affirmations for centuries.[3] And finally, it is experience itself which seems to speak most loudly about the mysterious blend of the divine and the demonic in creation. One has only to pick up a newspaper and read the headlines of the day to be reminded that there is evidence both of a righteous and omnipotent God and of an alien, evil factor at work in our world.

Rather than allow all three postulates to exist simultaneously, theologians, pastors, and sufferers have sought to relieve the tension, and thereby to solve the paradox of theodicy, by eliminating one of the three.

HISTORICAL ATTEMPTS TO RELIEVE THE TENSION

Eliminating "Evil is Real"

Christian Scientists under the leadership of their founder Mary Baker Eddy have sought to solve the paradox of theology by eliminating the third postulate—"Evil is real." The following premises seem to represent the basics of Christian Science:

> God is All;
> God is Mind; (therefore)
> Mind is All.

> Mind is All;
> Matter is not Mind; (therefore)
> Matter does not exist.

> God, Good, is the only reality.
> Sin and sickness are not good. (therefore)
> Sin and sickness are not real.[4]

Of course, logical syllogisms of this kind are only as valuable as the sum of their parts. Take any one postulate and disprove it (like the pantheistic assertion that "All is God"), and the entire structure comes tumbling down. Be that as it may, by arriving at the conclusion that matter does not exist, Christian Scientists also claim that pain, sickness, suffering, and death are both illusory and the result of false beliefs.[5] Try sharing the unreality of pain with one who has just unintentionally hit the thumb with the hammer, or experienced a root canal, or had back surgery. Or worse, try to inflict the unreality of death upon one whose parent has recently died.

The unreality of this attempt to relieve theodicy's tension is all too evident. It just doesn't square with life as we know it.

Eliminating "God is Good"

Anton LaVey has the dubious honor of representing those who have attempted to eliminate "God is good" from the triad of theodicy.[6] LaVey and his California-based Church of Satan published a satanic Bible in which most of the classic biblical texts have been either inverted or shamelessly revised. The final effect is one in which the good God becomes the evil God and vice versa. While LaVey's point is more hedonistic than scholarly, his legacy at the very least serves as an example of those who take issue with the notion of a benevolent Judeo-Christian God.

While God's righteousness is an important dynamic in the theodicy dilemma, the issues surrounding "God is great" (God's omnipotence) are even more crucial. Over and over in the course of ministering to suffering hospital patients as a chaplain and then as a pastor, I have discovered that most people seem to struggle more with what appears to be God's powerlessness than with God's ceasing to be good and positively disposed toward them. They wrestle with, "Why does a God who is able to do anything not do something for me?" Sometimes this can develop into the patient's calling into question his or her own righteousness. In my experience the patient does not don't usually question God's righteousness, however, but is more likely to say, "God's not doing anything to help because I'm a terrible sinner," rather than "God is evil."

Eliminating "God is Great"

Rabbi Harold Kushner, in his popular book *When Bad Things Happen to Good People*, seeks to alleviate the tension of theodicy by eliminating "God is great" (God's omnipotence) from the triad. Although I gladly give him credit for his willingness both to "take theodicy on" and to be vulnerable about his own painful struggles with the issue (Kushner tragically lost his son to progeria, the premature aging disease), the book is not without its weaknesses. The following quotes are representative of his position throughout the book. The first is based upon Kushner's interpretation of the book of Job.

> Let me suggest that the author of the Book of Job take the position which neither Job nor his friends take. He believes in God's goodness and in Job's goodness, and is prepared to give up his belief in proposition (A): that God is all-powerful. Bad things do happen to good people in this world, but it is not God who wills it. God would like people to get what they deserve in life, but He cannot always arrange it. Forced to choose between a good God who is not totally powerful, or a powerful God who is not totally good, the author of the Book of Job chooses to believe in God's goodness.[7]

Kushner uses an additional illustration to make his point.

> If we have grown up, as Job and his friends did, believing in an all-wise, all-powerful, all-knowing God, it will be hard for us, as it was hard for them, to change our way of thinking about Him (as it was hard for us, when we were children, to realize that our parents were not all-powerful, that a broken toy had to be thrown out because they *could not* fix it, not because they did not want to). But if we can bring ourselves to acknowledge that there are some things God does not control, many good things become possible.[8]

I would submit that while Kushner's line of argument does move us happily away from a worldview that places the responsibility for everything that occurs in the world and universe with God (a kind of theological determinism), the problems that result from casting aside God's omnipotence outweigh the benefits.

There are a number of ways Kushner's work might be critiqued. One might criticize him, as does Beker, for his rather careless use of the words *good* and *bad*.[9] Douglas John Hall also notices this tendency and wonders who and what Kushner has in mind when he speaks repeatedly of good people, not to mention bad things.

> For the world is not so easily divisible into good and bad. Are the "bad" things that happen to good people so obviously bad always? . . . More important, are the people—including Job—so obviously good?[10]

One could also critique Kushner from a philosophical perspective and point out that his eliminating God's omnipotence "courts a cosmic dualism."[11] Kushner's tendency in this direction becomes all the more evident as he continues to emphasize the chaotic element in the world.

It is also unfortunate that, in spite of the fact that Kushner says he wants to preserve goodness and love as attributes of God, the tone of his book is one in which God's love and mercy seem strangely lacking. He leaves us with the sense that God is not proximate but distant and somewhat removed.

While there exist many other potential avenues for critique, I am most interested in the effects that the elimination of God's omnipotence might have on the faith and psyche of a sufferer such as a seriously ill hospital patient. I would submit that Kushner's formulations compromise three rather major sources for faith and hope amidst suffering: Scripture, prayer, and worship.

The hypothetical scenario is this: I, the pastor, have just told Ms. Smith, my parishioner, that "the reason God does not seem to be helping" (which is her tearful complaint) is that her lifelong conception of God as being powerful and omnipotent needs revision. "God is good and loving, but not powerful," I assure her. "God would like to help, but can't." I then go on to share several insights from *When Bad Things Happen to Good People* and from the Bible, noting some places where it appeared that God could not help (Paul's thorn in the flesh, the disciples' inability to heal a young boy).

Following several winces intermingled with frowns, as if to say, "I asked for bread and you gave me a stone," Ms. Smith proceeds to cite a list of Scripture texts which do indeed seem to speak of a God who is creator, redeemer, conqueror, majestic and mighty, present in times of trouble, high and lifted up and powerful.[12] I squirm as I suddenly realize how important not only the Scriptures are to her, but how important those attributes of God are for her, especially at a time like this. It doesn't seem appropriate to continue the discussion any further. After fumbling a bit with some closing remarks intended to provide support, such as, "I'll come see you again sometime," I sense that it's time for me to leave.

As I stand up to leave, Ms. Smith makes a final request. "Would you say a prayer before you go, Pastor?" I respond, "Sure, I'll say a prayer," wondering in my mind what on earth I am going to pray *for*. Should I honor her belief that God is still powerful and mighty and high and lifted up? Or should I be true to my own belief that God is not powerful? I decide to pray with integrity. "O God, thank you for the blessing of medical science. We trust in their skills and wisdom. Please guide the hands of the surgeons as our sister experiences their healing touch tomorrow morning. And through this difficult experience help us to find some kind of meaning. Amen." I shake Ms. Smith's hand and make my exit.

Not wanting to be overly facetious, I am trying above to illustrate how different a pastoral care interaction would be if traditional biblical themes and images of God's omnipotence were eliminated. What scriptural assurances are left to provide comfort? Even those texts that indicate God's care, presence, and love are jeopardized if God is stripped of suprahuman credentials. God's presence is rendered no more special than that of the nurse, doctor, or chaplain. Without detracting in any way from the significance of these health care professionals, I do want to emphasize the unique and significant quality of the presence of God.

As was illustrated in the pastoral interaction above, a myriad of biblical texts that point to a powerful God are brought into serious question. Kushner does not offer any suggestions as to how those whose belief systems will not allow them merely to ignore blocks of material from an authoritative book should handle this dilemma. This issue needs to be reckoned with at some point. The hospital room, as in the example above, is never an appropriate place to hold a "corrective" Bible study, however. Even if one does have some fundamental disagreements with a patient or parishioner's theology, we do them a grave disservice if we ask an already tested and in some cases even battered faith to bear up without the benefit of lifelong beliefs and affirmations. This was the case for Ms. Smith above. Hall says it best when in speaking about the sufferer he reminds us that:

> Biblical faith has learned from the biblical God that the one who fell among thieves is more important even than our most precious theological assumptions and religious obligations.[13]

Did not prayer become a very different experience, in the above example, when God could not be spoken of or to in terms of power, majesty, or direct help? One would wonder how to pray, as did the attending pastor. When Jesus' disciples asked him, "Lord, teach us to pray," he responded with a model prayer that, "according to other authorities, some ancient,"[14] specifically made reference to the power of God: "For thine is the kingdom and the power and the glory. . . ." Power is such an integral part of how we have been taught to conceptualize God that to dispense with it would reduce prayer to a weak and benign enterprise of stating the obvious and hoping for the best from the powerful "gods" of medical science and human reason. This is prayer wrongly directed and gone amok, especially in situations like that of Ms. Smith, who had the expectation (though it was not stated explicitly, but implicitly) that her minister would direct the prayer to God rather than to the power of her doctors.

The hypothetical scenario continues, and Ms. Smith happily recovers and returns to her home and eventually to church. After several Sundays of attendance, however, she makes an appointment with me, her pastor, with complaints of being unable to worship. "You see," she explains, "I got to thinking about what you told me in the hospital about God not being the way I had always thought. Your insights about God not being powerful satisfied my quandary then, but now that I am home I don't know how to pray or worship. I'm so confused."

Worship is an act of expressing "worthship"[15] and significant value to a person or power we deem beyond us—"wholly other."[16] Kushner's powerless God lacks the aboveness and otherness that is necessary in order for worship to maintain its transcendent quality. It is no wonder that Ms. Smith had difficulty. She was attempting to worship one who was no more beyond her than her next-door neighbor. Her pastor "solved" the dilemma she faced in the hospital as she struggled to explain why it felt as if God was not helping her, but now that same "answer" had come back to haunt her *and* her pastor.

I believe that Rabbi Kushner genuinely seeks to comfort and assist persons who experience "bad things" in life—tragic suffering. It is the way in which he leads us out of the formidable maze of theodicy, however, that is found lacking. Indeed, he relieves the tension of the ancient paradox by eliminating the postulate, "God is great." But as I have outlined above, he causes more harm than good to the belief systems of persons who so rely upon this notion of omnipotence as it is presented in Scripture and utilized in prayer and worship. And it is especially the case with persons experiencing serious illness that this notion of a powerful God becomes all the more significant. Suffering persons need to have at least a few mainstays in the midst of their storms. In my experience with patients, a powerful God becomes someone they can hold on to when "all around is sinking sand."

But it is not as if I am sensing a spiritual and emotional need in human beings and then, after the fact, seeking to fabricate some means by which they might have that need satisfied in a belief in a powerful God! No, God is characterized this way in the ancient Scriptures and teachings of Christianity. God has revealed Godself as the omnipotent and powerful One. It is on the basis of such revelation that theologians have wrestled for so long with the issue of omnipotence versus evil. While I would add that I think this doctrine of omnipotence has been subject to abuse and misunderstanding and that it is in need of reinterpretation, I am not prepared to toss it overboard in the course of seeking simple answers to the theodicy problem. It would seem that the burden should *not* be upon those who wish to maintain such an attribute but upon those who submit that we should no longer think of God in these terms. Kushner's argument against omnipotnece is unconvincing at best.

In addition to needing a sense of anchoring amidst suffering, sufferers also need to have some basis for hope. I believe one of the key sources for hope is a belief in a suprahuman, "wholly other," powerful God. Trust and belief in this kind of a God can not only produce a sense of security in the moment but a vision of future hope. This kind of vision is lacking from Kushner's work. He gives no basis upon which a person can look beyond the present dark moment. All he has to offer is human resources, with "God's help," leaving it up to us to look for some kind of meaning in the suffering.

> Let me suggest that the bad things that happen to us in our lives do not have a meaning when they happen to us. They do not happen for any good reason which would cause us to accept them willingly. But we can give them a meaning. We can redeem these tragedies from senselessness by imposing meaning on them.[17]

And this:

> How does God make a difference in our lives if He neither kills nor cures? God inspires people to help other people who have been hurt by life, and by helping them, they protect them from the danger of feeling alone, abandoned, or judged.[18]

Because of Kushner's deficient grasp of God's omnipotence, the sufferer's resources are narrowed dramatically. God's involvement becomes rather diffuse, leaving us no alternative but to place our dependence squarely upon the shoulders of humanity. While there is certainly some truth to be found in the comments Kushner makes regarding the sufferer's responsibilities to seek for meaning and look to the support of other human beings, futility sets in if God's transcendent presence is absent.

It has most likely become quite clear to the reader by now that the present writer feels committed to preserving omnipotence as an attribute of God. I have based my case against dispensing with omnipotence on the biblical, emotional, and pastoral care concerns above. So at this juncture the question becomes one of methodology. How do we conceptualize the power of God?

I shall take an important methodological cue from Douglas John Hall, who I believe says it best: "Every responsible attempt to rethink the question of God and human suffering must involve in a primary sense a radical reinterpretation of divine omnipotence."[19]

I believe Hall is very much on target here, and it is in precisely this direction that I plan to proceed. Rather than eliminating "God is great" from the paradoxical triad of theodicy, a way must be found to preserve its place in describing who God is, while at the same time not falling into the deterministic pit that Kushner sought so diligently to avoid.

Karl Barth, one of the more influential theologians of our century, defined power christologically. That is to say, rather than eliminating "God is great" from the paradoxical triad of theodicy, Barth redefines power in a way that is able to preserve its place in describing who God is, by defining the character and nature of power as presented in the life, death, and resurrection of Jesus Christ.

Although Barth today is more significant to some than to others, I believe he has much to offer when it comes to issues surrounding theodicy. In fact, I think it is safe to say that Barth "shines" in this regard. It is to Barth's contributions that we will now turn.

5

KARL BARTH SPEAKS
OUT ON EVIL

Bill Johnson, a parishioner from your church, has called to ask if you would meet him at the local hospital's emergency room. When you arrive you learn that his spouse and young daughter are in critical condition following a hit-and-run motor vehicle accident. Bill sobs and questions, "Oh why, why?" You, his pastor, respond, "Well, in the words of a favorite rabbi of mine, I guess we can chalk it all up to God's powerlessness and our need to attach some meaning to this tragedy."

OMNIPOTENCE AND INCARNATION

Does a pastor not have any consolation to offer a suffering parishioner beyond "God can't help you" and "The best we can do is rely on our humanity"? To this question Barth would answer an unequivocal yes. In his valuable section in his *Church Dogmatics* entitled "The Way of the Son of God into the Far Country," Barth defines power in a way that is able to preserve this attribute in describing who God is, by interpreting the character and nature of power through the incarnation, suffering, and death of Jesus Christ.

According to Barth we see God most fully in the person of Jesus. It is when God takes on flesh and blood, hands and feet, that we begin to understand the nature of God. From Barth's perspective, attaching *a priori* attributes to God based upon the presupposition that there is a natural correlation between human beings and God (*analogia entis*) is not a healthy starting point. He contends that the Word of God, as seen through eyes of faith, is the only proper object and starting point for theology.[1] Thus we begin to have a sense for Barth's christological focus.

For Barth the incarnation is absolutely basic and crucial. It is in the life, suffering, and death of Christ that something very poignant regarding the nature of God is revealed. Speaking specifically of God becoming flesh, Barth states:

> If we think that this is impossible it is because our concept of God is too narrow, too arbitrary, too human—far too human. Who God is and what it is to be divine is something we have to learn where God has revealed Himself and His nature, the essence of the divine. And if He has revealed Himself in Jesus Christ as the one who does this, it is not for us to be wiser than He and to say that it is in contradiction with the divine essence. We have to be ready to be taught by Him that we have been too small and perverted in our thinking about Him within the framework of a false idea of God.[2]

What Barth is proposing here is truly new from the standpoint of "the old orthodoxy," not to mention the private theologies of us all. In essence he sets free the notion of true deity. For if God is God, should not an integral part of "Godness" be existence in a dimension far removed from that which can be totally understood and grasped by human beings? How presumptuous of us to assume that God's ways are our ways, or worse, that God should never venture beyond the bounds of human reason's ability to grasp God. Such thinking thwarts our true understanding of God's sovereignty, as it implies that God's righteousness and power, too, can be conceptualized in human terms. Barth restores for us a sense of God's transcendence, without which our concept of the immanence of God would suffer. Allow me to expand on this by referring us again to Ms. Smith, the hospital patient.

The very reason Ms. Smith and the majority of suffering people desire that God be close to them in their time of need is their belief that God, as God, is at a very basic level "far" from them. Immanence and transcendence go hand in hand. What kind of a God would Ms. Smith want to be close to her? The kind of God who could genuinely help. And a sovereign, transcendent, and omnipotent God can help, support, heal, and be ultimately personal because this kind of a God has the resources and power so to do. Barth places before humanity a God who is by nature removed, but is in practice pursuing, intimate, and close.

It is in the incarnation, according to Barth, that this mighty God illustrates both transcendence and immanence. Yet upon closer inspection, what is revealed about God in Christ is truly scandalous from the perspectives of old orthodoxy and classical theology.

In other words, it is true, but in hiddenness, in a way which is unexpected, which is new in relation to all general concepts of God and those concretely delivered in other places, in a way which is not perceived or known. The Almighty exists and acts and speaks here in the form of one who is weak and impotent, the eternal one as one who is temporal and perishing, the most high in the deepest humility. The holy one stands in the place and under the accusation of a sinner with other sinners. The glorious one is covered with shame. The one who lives forever has fallen a prey to death.[3]

What do we learn about God in that context in which God is most fully revealed—the incarnation? Barth identifies several startling insights. First, we discover that which is "unexpected." It is hard for us to imagine that God could, based on human notions of deity, enter our dimension of time and space. Is this not inconceivable? Our minds are possibly able to grasp the idea of a transcendent God, and perhaps even of an immanent God, but not a God who achieves both.

Second, based on our traditional categories, it is stressful for us to begin to conceive of God being humbled as a "sinner" standing with other sinners. It is one thing for God to gaze down upon us miserable sinners with pity and love from afar. It is quite another for the Righteous One to become one of us. This is too self-effacing an act for our sensibilities to bear.

In addition, it is almost impossible for us to fathom how a God who has been classically defined as being "impassible," that is, insulated from pain, could, in Barth's words, have "fallen a prey to death." It is rather unthinkable that the eternal God would choose to succumb to the power of brokenness to the point of tasting the same death that we taste.

And finally, this God whose omnipotence Barth so wants to preserve is seen in the incarnated yet vulnerable Christ as "weak and impotent." Does this then indicate that God has indeed been mistakenly clothed with omnipotence by the biblical writers and the theologians throughout the centuries, as Rabbi Kushner would argue? To arrive at this conclusion would be to miss Barth's point entirely.

Two important comments need to be made at this juncture concerning Barth's theology. First, Barth's vision of God becoming flesh can be termed in my mind "radical incarnation." He takes very seriously the

Apostle Paul's affirmation that "God was in Christ reconciling the world to Himself."[4] Christ, in Barth's thinking, *is God*, and through Christ God becomes experientially one with humankind. A bond of ultimate solidarity is achieved through the incarnation. Thus, as Jesus was rejected, God was rejected; as Jesus wept, God wept; as Jesus experienced profound suffering, so also God experienced the same.

What a contribution is made herein to the field of practical and pastoral theology! Such a vision of incarnation has tremendous implications for the ministry that pastors, chaplains, and lay persons alike seek to provide to the needy. In this incarnational light God can no longer be viewed as the High and Mighty One, insulated from the woes of the human plight, in which the traditional theology of the centuries would have us believe. Barth's theology is revolutionary. The "old wineskins" are no longer able to bear these revolutionary concepts. Suddenly we catch a glimpse of a God who loves us so much that God chooses to identify totally with humanity. This commitment then thrusts God into our own arena of brokenness and suffering, causing God to experience firsthand our human condition.

Those seeking to minister, then, can bring to the victims of tragic suffering the consoling news that God can help "when bad things happen to good people," because God has truly been in their place. God can help because God understands at a profound level what it means to sense alienation, suffer pain, and even face death itself. How powerful the presence of a God who has walked "through the valley of death" can be for one whose personal valley is dark and deep indeed! I will further expand on the implications of this dimension in the chapter that applies Barth's theology to pastoral care.

A second crucial issue needs to be highlighted at this point in Barth's reinterpretation of omnipotence. As I said above, Barth does not, dispense with God's omnipotence. Rather, he redefines it based upon what is for him the ultimate revelatory event—the incarnation. Speaking of God in Christ, Barth states that "the Almighty exists and acts and speaks here in the form of one who is weak and impotent."[5] In one sentence, Barth utilizes two key concepts: "the Almighty," which is a title indicating omnipotence, and "weak and impotent," which communicates the opposite of omnipotence. In this one seemingly paradoxical phrase Barth provides important insights into the nature of God's power and the way in which omnipotence and impotence are related in God. Impotence becomes the very channel through which God displays God's omnipotence.

> Who the one true God is, and what He is, i.e., what is His being as God, and therefore His deity, His "divine nature," which is also the divine nature of Jesus Christ if He is very God—all this we have to discover from the fact that as such He is very man and a partaker of human nature, from His becoming man, from His incarnation and from what He has done and suffered in the flesh. For—to put it more pointedly, the mirror in which it can be known (and is known) that He is God, and of the divine nature, is His becoming flesh and His existence in the flesh.[6]

And this:

> The New Testament tells us that it is essential and necessary for the one true God whom it finds in the man Jesus Christ to act and to reveal Himself in this way, to take this form in the coming of His kingdom and the accomplishment of the reconciliation of the world with Himself, in this way to be in the world and for the world the Almighty, the Eternal, the Most High, the Holy One, the Living One, the Creator, the Lord.[7]

From these quotes two issues become apparent. First, for Barth, incarnation is the focal point wherein we see God most clearly portrayed. It is also that place in which we learn most about God's omnipotence. And second, what we learn about God's omnipotence as it is displayed in the incarnated Christ forces us to reinterpret everything we would normally equate with omnipotence. For it is precisely in the weakness and vulnerability of the incarnation that God's omnipotence, interpreted christologically, is most clearly portrayed.

> God shows Himself to be the great and true God in the fact that He can and will let His grace bear this cost, that He is capable and willing and ready for this condescension, this act of extravagance, this far journey.[8]

"THE FAR COUNTRY" ILLUSTRATION

Barth uses an image from the parable of the Prodigal Son[9] to illustrate further his theology of incarnation and reconciliation. In this parable, Jesus tells a story of a man who had two sons. The younger son decided to leave the family business and strike out on his own. In order to do this he requested that his father give him his inheritance early. His father honored his wish and his son left home and journeyed "into the far country." After a long and difficult struggle in which he ran out of "play" money and took employment feeding swine that he too might eat, he "came to himself" and decided that he would rather work as a hired hand for his father than continue to experience the woes of the far country. The parable draws to a close in a tender scene in which the father and son are reconciled.

Barth draws a parallel between the father and son of the parable and God the "Father" and Christ the "Son." If we press the illustration too far, however, the similarities rapidly break down. For instance, even though the far country of the parable was a land quite different from that to which the young son was accustomed, and the world must have been similarly foreign for Jesus on some level, the latter did not succumb to the temptations of that far country. The young son of the parable is said to have been overcome by that country's power, as it was there that he "squandered his money in loose living."

An additional disjuncture between the experience of Christ and the son of this parable lies in what was behind their intentions for leaving "home" in the first place. The son of the parable journeyed into the far country seeking adventure, excitement, and self-gratification. Christ, on the other hand, came into *our* far country, the world, seeking not to be served but to serve. He was sent into the world on a mission of sacrificial reconciliation.

Another difference between this "prodigal" son and Jesus is that the former did indeed need to be reconciled to the father he dishonored. The relationship between Jesus and his "father" was in no need of mending. Jesus was God's beloved in whom God was well pleased.[10]

Several other points of divergence certainly exist between these two "sons," yet the main thrust of the parable does shed light upon the meaning of incarnation, which led to reconciliation. Regarding the far country to which Christ journeyed, Barth states:

In the fact that God is gracious to man, all the limitations of man are God's limitations, all his weaknesses, and more, all his perversities are His. In being gracious to man in Jesus Christ, God acknowledges man; He accepts responsibility for his being and nature. He remains Himself. He does not cease to be God. But He does not hold aloof. In being gracious to man in Jesus Christ, He also goes into the far country, into the evil society of this being which is not God and against God.[11]

Thus we can again see the kind of "radical incarnation" Barth wants to embrace. This is an incarnation in which God in Christ truly enters the far country and experiences all the evils of the far country without, importantly enough, being destroyed by those evils. In fact, the opposite occurs. God overcomes the powers of evil in the very act of experiencing them firsthand.

This again is such a helpful image for one who is bearing the brunt of suffering. "God does not hold aloof." God goes into the far country, a place that is far in terms of its being alien to God's dimension, and far in terms of the sacrifices which this costly journey involved. But the bottom line is that God in Christ has been here—that is, to the far country which is our "home" country—and God has known the suffering we know. And in a sense, through the Spirit, God has never left. God continues to be present to us amidst the suffering we experience. Pain is not new to God.

What a word of comfort and grace to Ms. Smith in her hour of need. Instead of trying to explain power away, it can be redefined through the powerful way in which God has profoundly identified and continues to identify with us. Such an identification is not theoretical. It is backed up by experience. "God has been where you are, Ms. Smith. And because of that, God is able to be here with you now."

Again we return to Barth:

> What marks out God above all false gods is that they are not capable and ready for this condescension, this act of extravagance, this far journey. In their otherworldliness and supernaturalness and otherness, etc., the gods are a reflection of human pride which will not unbend, which will not stoop to that which is beneath it. God is not proud. In His high majesty He is humble. It is in this high humility that He reconciles the world to Himself.[12]

This is power indeed. This is omnipotence determined not by the trait of aloofness, nor by the condition of being protected from harm. No, this kind of power had the ability to bend, to reach down, to do what needed to be done which no one else could do—in order to redeem humankind.

In a modern world in which even the church is adrift in its quest to define how its institutions and leaders should wield and express their power, it would be worth our while to look at the Christ event. For it is here that "servant leadership," a term that has become popular in theory but difficult to live out, is most clearly seen. Herein lies God's definition of power. For in Christ the omnipotence of God was pleased to dwell in humility and generous giving.

Ought this not then be a model for what the pastor should be like? In Christ we see a power that came to serve and not be served; to give glory to another (God) and not receive glory for himself. (So often it is the attention and honor that we pastors thrive on in our ministerial roles.)

And finally, in Christ what triumphed over "nothingness" and evil was not a thermonuclear fiat or an omnipotent aloofness, but a quiet yet determined act of self-sacrifice. If the church is looking for an insight into the nature and function of power, it need look no further. God becoming incarnate and then active in the life, death, and resurrection of Jesus Christ—this is the kind of power that redeems, brings meaning, and enables wholeness.

The church looks to the arenas of American politics and business, and to the systems of authority that other cultures offer, for clues as to what sort of character ecclesiastical or pastoral power should take. But no other model will do except the model that God places before us in Christ. Only in him is the true nature, genuine embodiment, and real source of power to be found.

NOTHINGNESS

While Barth's christological reformulation of God's power represents a significant contribution to the theodicy debate, I would be remiss if I did not introduce the reader to the term he uses to describe universal evil—"nothingness."

It is Barth's contention that the "older orthodoxy" was missing a link in its efforts to deal with the relationship between a good and powerful God and the evil that was an inherent part of the experience of humanity. In Christ, God bridges the experiential gap.

> The older orthodoxy did not make use of the simple and obvious possibility of considering this matter from a Christian standpoint, but treated creator, creature, and their co-existence and the intrusion upon them of the undeniable reality of nothingness, as if they were philosophical concepts which had to be resolved or brought into tolerable relationship.[13]

"Nothingness," for Barth, is that from which universal evil and tragic suffering stem.

> There is in world-occurrence an element, indeed an entire system of elements, which is not comprehended by God's providence in the sense thus far described, and is not therefore preserved, accompanied, nor ruled by the almighty action of God like creaturely occurrence. It is an element to which God denies the benefit of His preservation, concurrence and rule, of His fatherly lordship, and which is itself opposed to being preserved, accompanied and ruled in any sense, fatherly or otherwise. There is amongst the objects of God's providence an alien factor. . . . This opposition and resistance, this stubborn element and alien factor, may be provisionally defined as nothingness.[14]

Nothingness does not exist in the same sense that God and humanity exist. Yet neither is nothingness "nothing."[15] Nothingness is not a second god, nor is it dualistically self-created. It is not a part of the creation that God deemed "good." It is an alien factor.

Barth is the first to admit that his formulations of "nothingness" are fraught with paradox. This in his mind is appropriate. Regarding nothingness in particular, as well as all theology in general, Barth cogently reminds us: "All theology is *theologia viatorum*," which translated means, "All theology is a theology of pilgrims,"[16] pilgrims who "see through a glass darkly." We would do well to remind ourselves of this truth. Whenever we speak about God, whether it be from the pulpit or at the bedside, we should do so with humility, for we all grope together. Since this is the case, the pastoral carer has as much to learn from the reflections and struggles of the parishioner as does the parishioner from the pastor.

Barth says of nothingness that

> we have here an extraordinarily clear demonstration of the necessary brokenness of all theological thought and utterance. . . . It is broken thought and utterance to the extent that it can progress only in isolated thoughts and statements directed from different angles to one object.[17]

Barth continues to refine the rather elusive and paradoxical nature of nothingness by approaching it from several other angles. Nothingness exists on a different ontological plane than does God and the rest of creation. As an alien factor, it only exists because "God wills and therefore rejects what He does not elect. God wills and therefore opposes what he does not will. He says yes, and therefore says no to that to which he has not said yes."[18]

Several questions must be raised at this point concerning the adequacy of Barth's formulation of evil. First, we see that he is attempting to preserve both the sovereignty and omnipotence of God while still acknowledging the existence of evil as an alien force. He is careful not to flirt with dualism, always stressing the point that nothingness not only falls under God's authority, but it is on a completely different ontological footing from that of God and creation. Barth also avoids giving nothingness any kind of personality. The closest he comes to giving concrete examples is the point in which he equates nothingness with the primordial chaos and void of Genesis 1.[19] Nothingness remains faceless and almost nameless.

It is here that Barth might be criticized. While he admits earlier that his definition of nothingness is necessarily characterized by "broken thoughts," paradox, and humility, the concept at hand almost seems to defy description. Barth so shades the meaning of the term *nothingness* that it would seem, to use John Hick's expression, to "die the death of a thousand qualifications." It takes on an oblique, quasi-existence at best.

While I certainly laud the importance of theoretical and philosophical terms in reflecting on and describing the mysteries of reality, I do not find nothingness to be a helpful contribution. This is especially the case when it comes to ministering to the victims of tragic suffering. How helpful was it for the pastor in the short case portrayed at the outset of this chapter to toss out this term in the emergency room? It raised more questions than it answered. How helpful would it have been if I had introduced Ms. Smith of the previous chapter to the category of "nothingness"? Would it have shed any light on her existential plight of serious illness even if I had accompanied my use of the term with an extensive explanation as to its meaning and supposed relevance? I think not.

John Hick critiques Barth's conception of "nothingness" coming to be in the mysterious process of God's election/rejection:

> In willing and affirming a good creation God has unwilled, or willed against, a contrary possibility, and has thereby given that which was rejected and excluded a negative but nevertheless virulent power over against the real creaturely world. This view may be criticized both from within Barth's own thought world, as an infringement of his ban upon

speculative theorizing, and from outside that thought world, as a naively mythological construction which cannot withstand rational criticism.[20]

One of the reasons why Barth's work is so widely read by pastors, whose work is by nature "praxis-intensive," is Barth's propensity toward a useful theology. His own pastoral experience tempered his thinking in that direction. "Nothingness" does not, however, seem to fit into his overall schema of usefulness. I do not find that it sheds much practical light on the theodicy issue.

And I suppose that it is here that the power of the three-tiered paradox of theodicy can be seen really to hamper Barth's work. He is forced to take a "yes–no," dialectical approach to discussing evil's existence for the sake of a higher priority—God's sovereignty. His formulations seem quite vague, but this is the price he is willing to pay in order for the "God is great" and "God is good" postulates to triumph over "evil is real."

Far from viewing God as being powerless in the face of nothingness, Barth contends that nothingness was defeated through Jesus Christ.

> It is only an echo, a shadow, of what it was but is no longer, of what it could do, but can do no longer, for the fact that it is broken, judged, refuted, and destroyed at the central point, in the mighty act of salvation accomplished in Jesus Christ, is valid not merely at that point but by extension throughout the universe and its activity.[21]

We see at this point that Barth wants to maintain God's power by both guaranteeing the subservience of nothingness prior to the cross of Jesus Christ, and by highlighting its sound defeat in that same cross. What of the status of nothingness following the cross? Barth explains:

> Nothingness may still have standing and assume significance to the extent that the final revelation of its destruction has not yet taken place and all creation must still await and expect it. But its dominion, even though it was only a semblance of dominion, is now objectively defeated as such in Jesus Christ.[22]

In Barth's view, the termination of nothingness will be fully revealed in the return of Jesus Christ. Yet "God thinks it good that we should exist 'as if' He had not mastered it for us—and at this point we may rightly say 'as if.'"[23]

It is here that I believe Barth makes a genuine contribution. He injects into the theodicy issue the forward-looking vision that Kushner's treatment of the issue seems to lack. Without falling into escapism, Barth provides all of us, and especially those who suffer, a glimpse of the future, when at the Second Coming Christ will totally destroy all remnants of evil or nothingness. This is such a key contribution of Barth's that it really demands a separate treatment. I will expand upon its significance in a later section.

While Barth makes a real contribution in establishing a vision for the future, he seems deficient when it comes to describing how exactly nothingness should be viewed in the present. He has been careful to avoid giving nothingness too much power, and he has told us that nothingness will be "no more" at the return of Christ, but I would contend that he has not given evil its proper definition in the present world in which we live. Saying as he does that nothingness is only an "echo," a "shadow," a defeated force that exists only "as if" it had not been mastered, Barth leaves us wondering about its true essence. Is nothingness *then ontologically weak, but experientially strong?* In the thinking of this writer, we cannot have one without the other. Evil either has some bearing upon the present experience of humanity or it does not.

The history of evil might be summarized in the following way based upon Barth: Even from the beginning of time evil had a kind of quasi-existence. This same "evil" was then defeated at the cross of Christ and will finally be destroyed when Christ returns. As to evil's present state, we must insert a question mark. Barth is unclear about the existential nature of evil.

While a theological system like Christian Science would urge us to ignore the effects of present evil, I seriously doubt Barth would agree with such an extreme. (Not only would this be an inadequate answer from a theological standpoint, it would also be inhumane from the perspective of the sufferer.) Yet he stresses the point time and again that evil has been soundly defeated in the cross.

Perhaps it is here, in Barth's formulation of the cross, that the inadequacy of his conceptualization of nothingness is brought to light. Does he not inadvertently use the all-encompassing power of the cross to minimize the present evil effects of nothingness? Does he really want to go to the extreme of saying that nothingness was totally and completely defeated at the cross? Might it not be possible to say instead that nothingness was disarmed yet not defeated at the cross, and that what human beings experience through suffering, today, is indeed a vestige of nothingness that was not defeated? We might then go on to say, as does Barth, that nothingness will be thoroughly eradicated at the Second Coming of Christ.

Thus I find Barth's formulation of nothingness inadequate, especially at the juncture of the cross. Additional light would have been shed on the nature of nothingness had he provided an ontological and experiential exposé of nothingness before and after the cross.

I have outlined above Barth's concept of "nothingness," along with several points of critique. I now move on to summarize what has been covered in this chapter.

SUMMARY

We recall, first, that for Karl Barth, all of theology has a christological focus. In fact, we cannot even speak about who God is aside from what we learn about God incarnate in Jesus Christ. Thus incarnation is the watershed for Barth. It is that place where God is most clearly seen.

When we speak about the attributes of God, therefore, we must not begin with human reason. We must not assume that there is any natural correlation between God's nature and that of human beings. Our pursuit of God must begin with faith, and faith must begin its task by looking at the Word of God. And what do we learn about God as seen in the life, death, and resurrection of Jesus Christ? Among the many insights we gain into the nature of God, we learn much about omnipotence. It might be more accurate to say that all of our human notions of omnipotence are called into question. Perhaps this is why writers like Rabbi Kushner have abandoned omnipotence. Our conceptions of it are too narrow, too human, too this-worldly. The kind of omnipotence modeled by God in Jesus is no less powerful than what we might imagine. In fact, this omnipotence was the very force that disarmed the power of "nothingness," Barth's term for evil.

Nothingness is not a second God, nor is it dualistically self-created; neither is it part of God's good creation. It is an alien factor from which natural evil and suffering proceed. Through the cross of Christ God destroyed nothingness. What remains of it presently is its semblance of power. It was at this point that I criticized Barth for his tendency to be vague about the true nature of nothingness. Barth does say, however, that nothingness will come to its complete demise at the Second Coming of Jesus Christ into the world. Upon this word of assurance is a basis for future hope.

Yet this is not Barth's only word of hopeful consolation. In his treatment of the "Way of the Son of God into the Far Country," Barth makes a case for "radical incarnation." God was *in* Christ according to Barth, and as such God experienced firsthand the sufferings and trials of our world, the "far country" in which we live. God lovingly chose to go to the point of tasting rejection, suffering, alienation, and even death in order that we might be freed from the powers of "nothingness" and evil. In Christ God displayed God's omnipotence by becoming weak and humble, vulnerable and impotent. Other gods could not bear such condescension, but God displays much about the true nature of omnipotence in this way. In fact, impotence becomes the very channel through which God displays God's omnipotence. This boggles the human mind, but also comforts it. For when we suffer we can be assured of God's empathic presence. For our omnipotent God is not an armchair carer. No, God has been in our place. And our God is not an aloof bystander, but one who promised that all will be made right in the end, and in the meantime God will be for us our accessible comforter.

Having summarized the key thoughts of Barth on theodicy, we will now examine the ways in which they might be applied to the practice of pastoral care.

6

PASTORAL CARE: WHERE THEOLOGY TOUCHES DOWN

POWER IN WEAKNESS

In 2 Corinthians 12:7-9, Paul relates an incident wherein he was suffering from an unnamed malady. He terms whatever it was "a thorn in the flesh." Presumably through prayer, Paul asked God "that it might leave" him. He made his request three times with no results. Yet God did respond to Paul with a weighty word of explanation. God stated in essence, "You were not healed, Paul, but my grace is sufficient for you, for my power is made perfect in weakness."[1]

God's response to Paul is highly significant. I think that it can be interpreted in two ways. Traditionally this verse has been taken to mean that our very infirmities provide God with an opportunity to show forth God's sustaining grace. In other words, a person who is able with God's help to tolerate suffering and endure the pain that suffering brings to bear on one is really a kind of witness to the quiet inner resources that come through faith in God. There is much truth to be found in this interpretation. Indeed, we do lend credence to God's ability to sustain us when we struggle with our infirmities with faithful resolve.

Yet another interpretation of "My grace is sufficient for you, for my power is made perfect in weakness" might be the following: God's power is displayed in weakness and is made perfect, or complete, in the face of weakness. In fact, weakness is the very channel through which God displays God's power, God's omnipotence. By now this phrase should be ringing forth with sure familiarity. This is Barth's conception of divine power.

How crucial it can be, then, for a critically ill hospital patient suddenly to realize that the weakness and vulnerability that they deem such an enemy is actually the medium through which God mysteriously displays God's power. God is there *in* the pain. God is present *in* their hopelessness. God can now be sought in the very chasm of suffering rather than outside it amidst some facade of revivalistic human victory. Suffering has ceased to be only a human experience. God has chosen through the incarnation to make suffering God's dimension also.

Again, rather than eliminating omnipotence as an attribute of God, this text from Corinthians serves to preserve it. In Paul as well as Barth we can see new possibilities for envisioning God's power. In the words of Douglas John Hall:

> The *mythos* of the suffering God—of the God who yearns parentally towards creation; of the God who is not power*less* but whose power expresses itself in the weakness of love: this, I believe, is not only a more *profound* image of God than Kushner's limited deity, it is also more accessible to the human spirit. For every one of us knows, if we've lived and loved at all, something of the meaning of *that* yearning, *that* weak power, *that* powerful weakness.[2]

Yet in addition to the Corinthians verse providing us with a new vision of God in suffering, it also shows us the way in which God communicates or makes God's power known to us. It is through grace: "My grace is sufficient for you."

I suggested earlier that it might be said to Ms. Smith that God has been there; that is, God has experienced suffering through the cross, and because of that God is able to be here with us. Inherent in this grace of God is God's ability to empathize. I do not use this term lightly but in its most profound sense. If we mean by "empathize" the capacity for participation, then surely this term can be used of God, for it has been my contention all along that the incarnation is that place in which we witness God's full participation in the human plight.

We will recall that empathy, as a category, occupies a major position in the thought of Thomas Oden on the theology and practice of pastoral care. Oden states:

> When the Apostles' Creed confesses trust in the one who was born of the Virgin Mary, and suffered under Pontius Pilate, was crucified, dead, and buried, it expresses a penetrating affirmation of God's determination to share fully in our human condition. This stands against the docetic view that Christ was never really born. The early church witnessed to the infinite scope of God's unconditional empathetic love.[3]

You will remember that Oden goes on to link his concept of empathy in a more practical way with incarnation and pastoral care. Hence empathy becomes

> the process of placing oneself in the frame of reference of another, perceiving the world as the other perceives it, sharing his or her world imaginatively. Incarnation means that God assumes our frame of reference, entering into our human situation of finitude and estrangement, sharing our human condition even unto death.[4]

Thus empathy, in its most profound sense, might be seen as the grace "which is sufficient." It is the way in which God communicates God's power to us in the midst of tragic suffering. In the words of Arthur McGill:

> The God revealed in Jesus Christ is not brute power raised to the nth degree. This God exercises his powerful love in giving, by how much he nourishes his creatures, by how fully he communicates his own reality to them.[5]

In saying "my grace is sufficient," God gives the sense that this kind of grace can sustain because it proceeds from an empathy born of experience. It comes as a result of pain suffered on a "far" journey, taken to "the far country."

It is at this point that we must again consider the whole question of pastoral posture when visiting the sick. As persons seeking to minister we must first deny ourselves, our opinions, our projections as to what the patient/parishioner "must be feeling" and seek to enter that person's frame of reference, that person's "far country." This requires self-emptying on our part. It calls for sacrifice at some level. The issue that must be kept foremost in our minds is one of purpose. We visit a suffering person not for our benefit, but for theirs. Seeking always to incarnate the great Visitor himself, we must go to give of ourselves, to serve.

As was stated earlier, this sort of attitude is quite different from the one that might suggest that the pastor enters a parishioner's hospital room in order to direct the parishioner's thoughts and feelings. I am not suggesting that the pastor or other visitor should avoid giving theological input. Thomas Oden attributes such reticence to an identity crisis among ministers today. He claims that

A major effort is needed today to rediscover and remine the classical models of Christian pastoral care and to make available once again the key texts of that classical tradition following about fifty years of neglect, the depths of which are arguably unprecedented in any previous Christian century.[6]

I agree with Oden that we clergy have too often capitulated to the concepts and terminologies of other disciplines to the neglect of our own. When we shirk our "classic tradition," we do a disservice to those who call upon us for the sole purpose of receiving consolation from the ancient faith.

A BASIS FOR FUTURE HOPE

Barth's eschatological vision serves as a basis for hope for those who tragically suffer. In his treatment of nothingness as described above, Barth stated that nothingness was destroyed in the "mighty act" of Jesus Christ. Yet for Barth this mighty act still has another "scene" or two left to be played out. Through the cross nothingness was defeated at its core, but remnants of this force still hamper creation. It is only when "the hour strikes when its destruction in the victory of Jesus Christ will be revealed"[7] that nothingness and all of its effects will be entirely done away with. The issue does not have to do with whether nothingness was actually defeated in the cross; the issue rather pertains to the revelation of this defeat.

It was along these lines that I criticized Barth for not taking nothingness and the suffering it produces seriously enough. "If it is truly defeated," a patient in the intensive care unit might ask, "then why does it feel as though it is so very much alive in *my* illness?"

While my concerns along these lines continue, I do not want to belabor the issue in this section. I would instead like to use this opportunity to focus upon the end-time dimensions of Barth's thought and the fruit these thoughts can produce in the way of hope. While I tend to place more emphasis upon eschatology in my own theologizing than does Barth, it is quite clear from his comments about the total annihilation of nothingness at the Second Coming of Christ that eschatology indeed plays a part in his theological schema.

Paul tells the Thessalonians that he wanted to explain some things about those who had died in order that they might not "grieve as others do who have no hope."[8] He then goes on to relate that Christ would bring those who had died with him at his return, and that there would ensue a great resurrection reunion and the ushering in of the end of all things.

It is important to notice in this verse that Paul does not say, "Do not grieve." No, Paul says, "Do not grieve as others do who *have no hope.*" Grief is a natural and very human response to the tragedies of life. Tears and mourning are an appropriate reaction to tragic suffering and death. Even though nothingness has been defeated and will be totally defeated in the end, suffering and death represent formidable losses, if not adversaries, for everyone. It is crucial that we grieve in the face of nothingness. Stifling this response for whatever reason can be dangerous to our physical, psychological, and spiritual well-being.

The thrust of Paul's comment does not have to do with grief, but grieving without hope. For Paul and Barth the foundation for Christian hope is in the cross, resurrection, and Second Coming of Jesus. At the cross nothingness and evil were defeated. But the resurrection serves as a kind of harbinger for the future. It serves as a bridge as it joins the past and present with eternity. In the words of J. Christiaan Beker, the resurrection

> is not merely God's confirmation of the meaning of the cross, that is, approval of a suffering Christ who allows himself to be shoved out of the world. Rather, the resurrection is an event which follows after the cross and signifies the "first fruit" of the final defeat of the power of death in the coming Kingdom of God.[9]

In this sense the resurrection becomes a transition point in which the future invades the present with meaning and hope. The resurrection of Christ as "first fruit" implies that more "fruit" will follow, namely, our own individual resurrections. In spite of the fact that this will all occur in the future, the knowledge of these things in the minds of Barth and Paul has the power to sustain those who are suffering in the present with the reassurance that the end of the story is with God. Being assured of these things can serve as a stronghold for the sufferer amidst the flood of doubt and uncertainty that almost always accompanies such seasons of darkness.

How might this be translated into a pastoral care situation? The answer is, in a fairly straightforward manner. The secret of establishing hope lies first and foremost in the establishment of vision. If a hospital patient sees only the ravaging effects of cancer and the sure possibility of death, then hopelessness and despair will most likely set in. Again, we must not confuse despair with grief. The seriously ill parishioner undoubtedly will, and should, experience periods of grief. Grief is healthy, though inherently painful. Despair, on the other hand, which is the result of hopelessness, is not only debilitating for the sufferer, but has also been found to sabotage the healing process if there be any chance of healing. "Giving up" can be hazardous to your health.

Persons who are experiencing genuine hopelessness may not desire at the outset to see their minister and may not even be interested in seeing their families. If they are willing to be visited, they may appear somewhat distant. They may present a flat affect. However, they may also spend a lot of time weeping uncontrollably, or exhibiting a kind of mournful withdrawal. It is difficult to predict exactly how a person going through such depths of despair will appear.

Despairing persons feel as though they do not have a future in this world or with God, and usually avoid speaking in those terms. The prophet's statement becomes all the more relevant: "Without a vision the people perish." Despairing people lack vision. That is their main deficit.

If a pastor decides to try to rekindle hope in a person who seems to be experiencing hopelessness, this effort should be done with "kid gloves." Persons in this state need to be emotionally and spiritually "shaken," but this must be done carefully by someone they trust. In fact, trust plays a key role in any intervention's effectiveness.

One might begin by expressing love and concern for the patient. If the person is really feeling "down," these words might appear to "roll off their back." Theological images might be shared concerning God's empathetic presence which, through the incarnation, was informed by the suffering of the cross. Jesus' humanity becomes all the more reassuring at these times. Knowing that he experienced pain, cried out, and wept can enable the beginning of a sense of connectedness to God that leads to hope. As one is speaking about these themes it is important that one not make it sound like a lecture. Humility and sensitivity are a must. It is a profound privilege to be in this sufferer's presence. Keeping these truths in mind can help set the tone.

Finally, moving slowly and carefully, it may also be important to share with them a portion of the larger picture. This larger picture reveals a God who has defeated evil in the powerful cross of Christ, gives us a vision of what shall be for us in the resurrection, and assures us that the end of the story will involve death being "swallowed up in victory."[10] God holds us in life *and* death, only to bring us back again into life. The closing act of the great play will reveal that nothing indeed could separate us from the love of Christ—not height nor depth, nor things present nor things to come, not life nor death.[11]

Sharing these thoughts and Scriptures might not appear to faze the sufferer initially. It may require several visits. It may require much ministry of presence—that is, being with that person in silence—before he or she is willing to respond, to ventilate, to suffer aloud.

On the other hand, some statement may jar the suffering individual. They may begin to cry or sob. They may respond angrily, with much bitterness. Yet if they are able to do so, this is in and of itself therapeutic, for perhaps what you have helped them to do is break the icy emotional, spiritual, and sometimes even physical incapacitation that despair imposes. You have helped them back toward the more therapeutic environs of grief by restoring some sense of vision. You have ministered to them by lending them *your* eyes. Through you they may have caught a glimpse of present or future hope, a vision that could either display itself in the ability to plod on in the therapeutic process or aid them in making their peace with the illness in a more intentional resignation. This is their choice based upon the realities of the prognosis, their energy level at the time, and how they might sense the Spirit of God leading them.

When it is all said and done the questions still arise, "Why does God wait so long to make that which is wrong right? Why not mercifully get it all over with?" These are tough questions. For Barth, God "thinks it good that we should exist 'as if' He had not yet mastered it for us—and at this point we may rightly say 'as if.'"[12] Unfortunately Barth does not expand on this statement. He leaves us with the rather oblique reference "God thinks it good. . . ."

I am not able, nor do I desire, to launch out at this point on a crusade to suggest what evil's virtues might be. For the sufferer, evil/nothingness is without virtue. And in Kushner's mind it is a mad and random process of "bad things" happening to people, any people.

Hall does not offer us an answer, but simply describes what he sees in light of the God he knows. He describes a God who, being personally involved in and committed to the historical project, must not superimpose upon it a finality that is wholly discontinuous with its course. Not *can* not, but *must* not! To do so would be in effect to cancel creation, to count it as a failed experiment, to start over again. Omnipotence must wait! That is, if it is an omnipotence of love.[13]

This concludes the section on how Barth's theology might be applied to the concerns of pastoral care. In the next chapter, through the use of several case studies, I will further illustrate how a reinterpreted omnipotence might be used in ministering to people in pain.

7

MINISTRY IN THE TRENCHES

A PASTORAL HOSPITAL VISIT

Background and Context

Jean Brown is a sixty-eight-year-old widow, diagnosed as having cancer. She has had a number of admissions in which her doctors have performed surgery, then radiation treatment, and now more chemotherapy. Ms. Brown's prognosis is not good, according to her doctors. They have recently given her just a few months to live. During this admission they have increased the potency of her chemotherapy treatments as an extreme measure to curb the progress of her cancer. These treatments have resulted in additional hair loss and bouts of nausea.

Ms. Brown has been a church member all her life. She is presently a member of a church that has a new pastor by the name of Steve Talbot. In fact, she is one of the first pastoral visits that he will make in his new position.

Ms. Brown's former pastor, Rev. Peterson, visited her quite consistently during her previous hospital admissions. He was a kindly man, but not at all comfortable with hospitals or suffering people. It seems that he, too, knew suffering, having just lost a family member the year before he accepted a call to another church.

During his last visit with Ms. Brown, the former pastor shared several thoughts with her from a book he was reading, *When Bad Things Happen to Good People* by Rabbi Kushner. As he found much of the Rabbi's thought to be on target, especially the suggestion that God was no longer omnipotent, he decided to share these thoughts with Ms. Brown. She found some of what he said to be troubling. While at home between hospital admissions she even made an appointment with her former pastor to discuss her struggles along these lines. This did not seem to help. She was confused by this "new" way of thinking about God.

During the present admission Ms. Brown is having an especially difficult time. She may very well not return home.

Rev. Talbot introduces himself to the nurses at the nursing station and checks to see if this is a good time to visit Ms. Brown. They assure him that she has had a difficult day, but that this is as good a time as any. He goes up and knocks at her door. She responds in a weak voice and he enters.

A Verbatim of the Visit

(M = minister; P = parishioner.)

M: Hello, Ms. Brown. My name is Steve Talbot. I'm the new minister at your church.

P: Yes, I know who you are. I've read about your coming in the . . . *[She begins to cough and grabs her tissue box and kidney pan.]* I'm so sorry. Excuse me. I've been so sick this time. Nothing seems to agree with me anymore.

M: Ms. Brown, if this is not a good time for me to visit, I can come back another time.

P: Oh no, please stay. That is, if you don't mind my sputtering and carrying on.

M: Not at all. I understand you're having a rough time of it.

P: Yes I am, but there are others a lot worse than I am. I'll make it.

M: Well, I imagine that there is always someone worse off if we look for them hard enough, but that doesn't detract from the horrible time I understand that you've had.

P: Well, I suppose not. This time has felt very different from other times. I've never been so sick and I don't know what's going to come of it. *[She starts to tear up and then to cry. She wipes her eyes.]*

M: I'm sorry that things have been so tough for you.

P: *[More tears]* Thank you. They are doing all that they can do. They're so good. I've gotten such good care here.

M: I'm glad to hear that. What did you mean when you said that this time it feels different?

P: *[Crying again and wiping her eyes]* Oh, I guess at times it just seems like I'm not getting anywhere. *[Silence]*

M: You mean that you're getting worse?

P: Yes, and I don't feel like God is helping me either [*crying through her words*]. Pastor Peterson—he was our former pastor—he and I had many talks about it, but they didn't seem to help. And I can't see boring you with it all. You probably have lots of better things to do with your time, just getting into town and all. When did you begin at the church?

M: Just this week, but I came over to spend some time with you; that is, if you are comfortable talking about such things with a complete stranger.

P: [*She smiles.*] Oh, it's fine. It's not that so much [*wiping her eyes some more*]. I've been wanting to meet you.

M: Well, I wanted to come over and meet you, too, Ms. Brown. I don't pretend to have all the answers, and maybe your talks with Pastor Peterson didn't help you very much. But I'm certainly willing to talk with you about anything.

P: There is one thing that really confuses me, and really did upset me for a time. Pastor Peterson and I were talking one time about God's power. I think I may have said something about God not feeling close to me or not helping me. Sometimes I get awfully blue. Well, anyway, you know what Pastor Peterson said?

M: [*He shakes his head.*]

P: He said that most people had the wrong idea about God, and that God wasn't powerful like we thought he was. How do you like that? [*said with consternation*]. He was reading some book about the reasons for suffering and he said that the author really helped him. Well, he didn't help me. Pastor Peterson lost his daughter over a year ago now, you know. I suppose we both are looking for answers.

M: Yes, that could very well be. The book you mention sounds familiar. It may be one by Rabbi Kushner called *When Bad Things Happen to Good People*.

P: Yes, that's it. It must be popular.

M: Yes, a lot of people have read it. In fact, it was on the bestseller list for a long time.

P: Have you read it?

M: Yes.

P: Do you agree with it?

M: I have mixed feelings about it. I think the author really does struggle with the issue. He had a tragic loss in his own life.

P: Yes, that's what I understand.

M: What are your own feelings about God's power, Ms. Brown?

P: Well, I grew up always believing in a powerful God. I was taught that in Sunday School also. But not only was I taught that God was powerful, the Bible says that God *is* powerful. It talks about a God who is creator, and about a God who is mighty and high and lifted up. How can anyone then say that God isn't powerful anymore? I just can't see it. *[She coughs some more and has to stop for a moment.]*

M: I, too, believe in a powerful God, Ms. Brown. However, I always want to be careful to make sure that my definition of power is in line with God's definition of power. A wise theologian by the name of Barth reminds us that we shouldn't put words in God's mouth. When we talk about what God is like we should go to the place where God is most clearly revealed, and that's in Jesus.

P: I agree with that, for in him the fullness of God was pleased to dwell. I memorized that a long time ago for Vacation Bible School.

M: That's right. That is an excellent verse for what I'm talking about.

P: But if God's not powerful, we're all sunk.

M: I agree. Except what kind of power do we see in Jesus?

P: He healed people. He did miracles. He even raised old Lazarus from the dead.

M: Right, he did all of that. Except we also see a Jesus who cried. Remember the shortest verse in the Bible? "Jesus wept."

P: Oh yes, I remember. *[Her eyes start to fill up with tears.]*

M: Jesus suffered and knew incredible pain, pain not unlike the pain you've felt. And Jesus also knew what it was like to feel lonely and alienated—far away from God. He cried out, "My God, my God, why have you forsaken me?" That's a different kind of power. It's a vulnerable and suffering power. But that kind of power is the very thing that defeated sin and darkness and evil on the cross. That suffering power changed the world. *[Pause]* I don't want to make this sound like a sermon.

P: No, I like what you're saying. That is a different way of looking at power.

M: Yes, it is. But I believe that this is what the Bible teaches us regarding power. This is God's power. *[Silence]* I sense you have been through a lot with your illness, Ms. Brown.

P: Yes, I have *[said almost confessionally]*. It has been a long time since I have felt like myself. I can get pretty down, you know.

M: Ms. Brown, it is pretty natural for a person who has been through as much as you have to get down. I know I would.

P: But it just doesn't feel right. I should have more faith, but it doesn't seem to come. I pray for God to help me, but the help doesn't seem to come. My prayers are not answered. What does that say about a powerful God? *[teary again]*.

M: I don't know what it says, but the sound of your voice tells me that it hurts very much. *[He is silent as she cries.]* A person comes to mind, Ms. Brown, who was in the same boat as you. He had an unspecified illness, a thorn in the flesh, which caused him pain and limited his life. Three times he asked God to heal him, but nothing happened.

P: Are you talking about Paul?

M: Yes, I am. Paul wasn't healed, was he? Was it because he lacked faith?

P: Well, I don't think so.

M: No, I don't either. Do you remember the rest of the story? God must have been aware of Paul's feeling upset or maybe even angry, for God responded, "My grace is sufficient for you for . . ."

P: ". . . my power is made perfect in weakness."

M: Yes. Paul was not healed but God assured him that the presence, strength, and grace of God would be enough to get him by. And because God has suffered, God can be with you in a way in which no one else can. God has been there, Ms. Smith. God's power is now displayed in identification with you. God cries and hurts with you. If this is not power at its best, than I don't know what power is.

P: I should trust God more. I should have more faith, I guess.

M: I don't think it depends on you. The power of God is here. And besides, I'm not sure that this is a good time for there to be a lot of "shoulds" in your life. If there are any "shoulds," this might be a time in your life when you *should not* force yourself to be a certain way. Maybe it's time to be a little kinder to yourself and more patient with yourself.

P: I try, but I guess it's just my nature.

M: Maybe so. *[Pause]* I wonder if you would be willing to try something, Ms. Brown.

P: Yes.

M: I wonder if you might try to recover some of the ways you used to think about God. You mentioned that you used to believe in a God of power. I think at this time especially, that it would be important for you to believe in the same powerful God that you used to. Except, sense God's power in places you may never have sensed it before. If it's true that God's power can be known and made complete in weakness, then feel the presence of God with you when you feel the weakest. God is there in the weakness. God is there in your suffering, for our God is a God of suffering. You don't need special faith to locate God. God is there in spite of how you feel and in spite of your faith.

P: God's power in weakness. I have not thought about God's power in that way before. It makes God seem a lot closer.

M: Perhaps you might view it as a new twist on a very old truth. An old truth that you have always held dear—a powerful God. You look tired. Your coughing seems to have calmed down a bit, though.

P: Yes, it comes and goes. Thank you for coming, pastor. I hope you will come again.

M: I will, and we'll talk some more. Why don't we have a prayer before I go?

P: Oh yes, please. *[He takes her hand.]*

M: O God, thank you for this chance for Ms. Brown and me to visit and share our lives. You know what she has been through. You know her pain and worry, for you have been here all along. And the reason why you can be with her in such a powerful way is that you yourself have known suffering through your Son Jesus. In fact, suffering and weakness are the very channels in which you reveal yourself. So help Ms. Brown to sense your empathizing presence. Help her to lean on you and to trust you. For you are there in the very midst of her life, giving her just enough grace to keep plodding on. In the powerful name of Jesus. Amen.

P: Thanks for coming. I will try to sense God's presence here.

M: Do, Ms. Brown. I'll look in on you again soon. Goodbye.

P: Goodbye, pastor.

In this verbatim, Rev. Talbot utilizes the Scriptures as both a word of comfort and as a theological corrective to what he perceives to be his parishioner's rather skewed view of God's power. He seeks to introduce her to a different dimension of power, not through his own experience or opinions but through what becomes for his parishioner a fresh, new interpretation of biblical passages she had known for a long time. The Word is her source of authority. Interpreting it and applying the Word to her needs and experiences in the hospital makes an impact. Such reliance upon a Word of God that speaks a dynamic and contemporary word to life as we know it is most Barthian. And it is in this sense that Barth can inform both the theory and practice of pastoral care.

A PASTORAL HOME VISIT
WITH ONE WHO IS ANGRY

Background and Context

Randy Jones is a fifty-five-year-old widower who has just lost his wife to leukemia. She had a long, difficult illness with numerous hospital admissions for treatment over a period of five years. At one point Sandy Jones did go into remission, a sixteen-month period that many of her church friends lauded as a permanent healing from God, but then she rapidly worsened and died within six months. She is survived by Randy and two teenage daughters.

Shirley Shipley has been pastor at Good Shepherd Church for seven years and has walked this arduous road of suffering alongside the Joneses. She was very much involved when Sandy was first diagnosed, and present in the hospital room when she died last week. This interaction occurs on the evening of the day following the memorial service at the church. After calling first to check on Randy's availability and willingness to receive a visit, Rev. Shipley rings the bell and is invited inside. The house is dimly, if not grimly lit. Randy invites his pastor to sit and they begin to converse.

A Verbatim of the Visit

(M = minister; P = parishioner.)

M: Thanks for letting me come by, Randy. I've had you and the girls on my mind quite a bit today.

P: Well, thanks for checking on us, and thanks for the good job you did at the service. Sandy would have been pleased with the way everything went; I know I was. *[Looking down-stated rather flatly.]*

M: *[After a pause]* Well, I felt privileged to do the service for you and for Sandy. She was a significant person to you and to all of us.

P: Yeah. *[Shaking his head]* But I can't figure it.

M: *[Silence]* Figure what?

P: *[Pause]* I can't figure out where God was when all this was happening. But you don't want to listen to all this. You've got a family to be with tonight rather than listening to my moans and groans.

M: Yes, I have a family, but tonight I came over to check on this family. What are you trying to figure out?

P: Well, the whole thing seems so cruel. Here Sandy was minding her own business, working, raising two girls, going to church, and leukemia invades our lives. So she gets treatment [said haltingly with the dry breath of intense emotion], the best treatment, and it works. God dangles healing before all of us and then snatches her away. What kind of a God does that? A God who is out to get us? *[Visibly angry now]* What did she ever do to deserve to die that way? *[Still looking down; elbows on knees; regularly wiping a tear from his eye.]*

M: *[Long silence]* I don't know Randy. *[Pause]* I don't have all of the answers about God. And maybe you're not really asking for me to answer.

P: No, I do want to hear what you think *[voice now rising in pitch]*.

M: *[Pause]* I sense your anger, Randy. I'm angry too and it's OK to feel put out with God. If we learn anything from the Psalms, we learn that God can take our anger. David ranted and raved and God could handle his honesty. God can handle ours also. *[Randy does not respond.]* *[After a pause]* Could it be, Randy, that God didn't assign Sandy leukemia, or cause it, or want to punish her in some twisted way? Could it be that we just live in a sick world where things like leukemia exist? A world even Jesus warned us about — "In the world you'll have tribulation, but be of good cheer. I have overcome the world." Right now there isn't much to cheer about because you're hurting; the girls are hurting; we're all hurting. But what I think happened to Sandy was not God's will but God's grief, like I tried to say in my meditation at the service. "Jesus wept," the shortest verse in the Bible, was a reality Saturday night in that hospital room. As we cried, so did the Lord.

P: But how about the false hope last year? *[Looking up, crying more profusely now.]* Why did God torture us with the hope that she'd make it? I'll never forget our trip to northern New England. She was so happy; we thought that we'd live happily ever after.

M: *[Pause]* I don't know why that happened, Randy. I know Sandy thought that trip was one of the highlights of your marriage, almost a kind of second honeymoon.

P: *[He looks up and interjects.]* I know, I'll never forget the look on her face when she saw the cabin. She had thought she'd never see it again.

M: She told me about that. It was an incredible high for her.

P: Yeah, but now it doesn't make much difference. It almost feels like we were set up.

M: *[Pause]* I can see how it might feel cruel to you Randy, but I glory in the fact that she was given that trip and those months of wellness. It was a gift.

P: *[He nods with a faint smile.]*

M: *[Long silence wherein they both just sit.]* Have we said enough for tonight?

P: I guess, I just miss her so. *[He weeps.]*

M: Yes. *[Allowing him to grieve.]*

P: *[After a long interval]* Please say a prayer for us.

M: OK, I will. *[Pause]* Dear God, please remind Randy and Susan and Elizabeth in the coming days, that as they weep, you weep; as they grieve, you grieve. Please help them to be patient with themselves and to lean upon one another and us as church friends, and yes, even you. I pray that you might reveal yourself as One who is neither a divine disciplinarian nor a sadistic God who assigns leukemia but as One who suffers with us when we suffer, and who suffered with Sandy during her brave struggles. We know Sandy is with you now. Please now help us to be with each other. Through Christ our Lord. Amen. *[Following a word with each of the daughters, Pastor Shipley takes her leave.]*

Randy Jones is not exactly over his angry feelings toward God. Neither will he ever entirely get over the loss of Sandy. Through three more weekly counseling sessions at the church office, however, Pastor Shipley is able to give permission to Randy to vent his feelings (especially his anger toward God) and, as a result, to begin to rebuild his faith. Reframing his image of God, not so much through directive teaching but nondirective queries (see the pastor modeling this during the first meeting—"could it be . . . ?"), was exceedingly beneficial to Randy as the pastor moved him from seeing God as punisher to experiencing God as empathizing companion.

A PASTORAL HOSPITAL VISIT
WITH ONES WHO ARE CONFLICTED

Background and Context

Alice and Jim Stiles have just lost their infant son, Christopher, who was born with severe genetic anomalies. Since his syndrome rendered him incompatible with life, the Stiles requested that the medical team remove him from the artificial life (as they called it) that the ventilator afforded.

Tom Bennett, Pastor of First Church, has been attentive to the Stileses throughout Alice's difficult pregnancy up to Christopher's birth. They have asked him to be present in the visitors' room of the intensive care nursery the evening they were to say their final goodbye to their son. Following that farewell they enter the room where Rev. Bennett has been waiting.

A Verbatim of the Visit

(M = Minister; A = Alice; J = Jim)

A: Hi, Tom [*as she sadly offers this greeting she slumps down into a chair weeping*].

J: Hi, Tom. [*Said with quite a bit more animation.*]

M: Hi, Alice, Jim [*almost a whisper*].

J: How's it going?

M: OK, OK. What was that like in there?

J: Oh, it was sad, yet reassuring that our Christopher is in a better place now. The Lord is with us.

A: Oh, it hurts so bad [*said between sobs*].

M: Yeah, I can only imagine. *[They all sit.]*

J: But, Honey, he's in a better place; he's with God now.

A: I know *[still weeping]*, but that's the worst thing I've ever had to do. It feels like my heart is being pulled out of me.

J: But we'll get over it *[patting her shoulder]*, just give it some time; you'll see.

M: You know, Jim, you're right. You will get on with your lives again, but the best way to do that is to let go now; to let go of the hurt and to cry and weep and acknowledge the pain.

[Pause; Alice looks over at Jim; he looks down.]

J: Instead of wasting a lot of energy on tears, I'd rather set my mind to try to figure out what God is teaching us through all of this. I know he's going to make us stronger, and that this thing didn't just happen. It happened because God wanted to get my attention.

A: Yeah, right *[responding to Jim]*; God took away our baby just to get our attention?! If that's the way God gets people's attention, then I don't want much to do with him. I can't believe we've gone through all this for that! *[Still crying.]*

J: But you can't say that. God has reasons that we don't know anything about or understand. We just have to thank him and praise him, right, Tom?

M: *[After a pause]* I don't know what we *have* to do at this point, Jim. I think the only thing we can do is grieve losing Christopher. Tell me what was going through your mind in there when you said your goodbye. What were you feeling? *[Alice is silent.]*

J: Well, you know I'm not very good at talking about my feelings. I was thinking about the disciples taking Jesus' body off the cross and placing him in the tomb. When we pulled the blanket up around and over Christopher's head and handed him to the nurses I felt like we were placing him in that tomb. *[First signs of emotion—a tear and a quivering chin.]*

A: I felt like we were handing the most precious thing in the world to God [sobbing again] and saying, "Here, you keep him for us." *[She buries her head in Jim's shoulder and he puts his arm around her, crying more openly now.]*

M: *[After a silence of two to three minutes]* You two have been through and will continue to go through one of the most painful experiences life can throw at us. And I don't have a sense that God willed this or wanted it. It happened, and God cries and grieves with us. For God knows what it's like to lose a son. *[Tom's eyes fill up with tears as he says these words.]*

J: God, how are we going to get through this? *[He maintains his embrace with Alice.]*

M: God will carry you through, Jim and Alice. And we who love you will also be there for you.

A: Thanks. *[She reaches out for Tom.]* We need you.

M: *[After an interval of silently sitting together]* May I say a prayer? *[They both nod.]* Dear God, please be present to Jim and Alice as they feel the pain of this loss. Christopher is precious to them and to all of us. We grieve that his little body was not able to go on, but we do have the assurance this night that his spirit is in your great big hands. That's a good place for him, but his absence here leaves us broken and at a loss. Help Alice and Jim to be patient with themselves over the difficult days ahead. And help them to share what's inside them with each other and with each of us. "When my heart is overwhelmed, lead me to the rock that's higher than I," prayed David. Amidst their being overwhelmed, be their rock, O God. Be an almighty, solid rock that they can lean upon. In Jesus' name we pray. Amen.

Pastor Bennett attempted to do a couple things in the interaction—encourage grief and offer a basis of hope. He sensed that Alice was experiencing healthy grief but that Jim was initially attempting to handle things cerebrally and theologically. Tom sought to move Jim away from the deterministic and didactic answers to a place where he might experience the empathy of God ("God knows what it's like to lose a son"). Jim seemed to get a glimpse of this as he related his story to Jesus' story. The tragedy of it all finally struck home, enabling him to join Alice. The pastor was also able to reinforce this couple's sense of hope, once he became convinced that Jim had moved to a more appropriate emotional place ("Christopher is in a better place" initially appeared to be rather escapist). His very intentional closing prayer summarized the two priorities he anticipated that he would need to address—grief and hope. Concerning future ministry to this couple, Rev. Bennett plans to follow up on both Alice's feelings toward God and Jim's seeming reticence to grieve.

8

NOW THAT THE FUNERAL'S OVER

While many pastoral carers indeed offer empathic, appropriate support to the bereaved immediately following a loss and extending right on through the funeral and beyond, the majority of us fall woefully short when it comes to long-term ministry. We tend to function on "red alert" during the crisis but then ease back into "holy neutral" during the ensuing months of mourning. Why such slackness? I believe much of it can be attributed to expectations—expectations of both our society at large, and, through contagion, clergy ourselves.

Most Westerners seem to be under the assumption that grief over a tragic loss should last a couple of days or, at the outside, a couple of weeks. We want people to "get over it" as quickly as possible so that we can be assured that they are "doing better," and so that we can all go on with our lives trouble-free, pain-free. This is both a tragic posture and a tragic conclusion, since, as it turns out, the mourning process takes months, if not years, to run its course, with numerous peaks and valleys along the way. And even then I would hasten to add that one never entirely "gets over" a tragic loss. The best we can hope for is that one will, over time and by the grace of God, learn to integrate the loss into one's daily life.

Dr. Glen Davidson, thanatologist, states that the first forty-eight hours to two weeks is critical for mourners as they experience the shock and numbness of their loss.[1] While any change in life carries with it the potential to disorient (that is, cause one to lose track of self in terms of person, place, and time), grief is debilitating to a much higher degree. Davidson's research indicates that disorientation for mourners peaks at forty-eight hours following the loss and again at significant anniversaries.[2] Yet he hastens to add that reorientation (that is, to sense release again, experience renewed energy, have the capacity for making good judgments, return to stable eating and sleeping habits), can take eighteen to twenty-four months—a duration quite foreign to our "quick fix" culture.

How might such data influence the practice of pastoral care? Significantly, I trust. In the first place, it should cause us to add a chronic dimension to our already acute understanding of the nature of grief, prompting us to view loss not so much as an event but as a process of long duration. Additionally, such thanatological data should motivate us to make an intentional connection with the bereaved at some juncture following the loss (perhaps at the six- to eight-week point), and especially at the important anniversaries for the bereaved (he or she being the one to guide you as to whether that particularly painful point will most likely occur on the loved one's birthday, a wedding anniversary, the anniversary of the death, or some other key date).

Besides these being supportive social calls, I would stress the importance of specifically naming the lost loved one and going on to explore how the loss is affecting life in the here and now. While it may be a temptation to keep the conversation free of pain and tears, in so doing we may also inadvertantly render the visit "therapeutic-free" and meaningless.

You might initially ask rather general questions, such as, "How are you doing, Bill?" or "What are you thinking about or feeling these days, Linda?" If these questions don't serve to induce the person(s) to give you a clear picture as to how they are truly functioning, or if you sense that they are putting "a good face on everything" for the sake of the pastor, you will need to ask some more specific questions about mood; about the times sadness typically descends; or about eating habits or sleep disturbances, if any. What you're after is a fairly holistic picture of life as it is for them in the longer term following the loss. Such gleanings will determine your next step, whether that be an additional follow-up visit, pastoral counseling, a referral to another helping professional, or simply periodic pastoral support. Just remember, if grief truly does peak around the time of this visit, then your mandate is to care in a way that is both clinically informed and empathically courageous. Visiting in order merely to discuss the weather is essentially a waste of everybody's time.

The other priority for me, especially around the one-year anniversary of the death, is to make what I might call a public intervention.

This would involve my reminding the church community of the loss or losses sustained over the months in the context of prayers or preaching so as to keep the process of grief alive on the corporate level. This not only enables us to resist the "quick fix" impulses of our society but also serves to garner the community's support for those who are still very much in the throes of grief.

On one occasion, when a year had elapsed since a particular parishioner had sustained the loss of his spouse, he and I met at the cemetery, at graveside, for a short service of remembrance, prayer, and the placing of flowers. As this anniversary was a peak grief time for this one particular sufferer, it was also a point at which pastoral care was particularly needed and appreciated. Let me add that in this instance, the parishioner initiated. We are oftentimes not so fortunate as to have one who can so clearly spell out his or her particular need and what role they would like us to fill; thus the necessity of tracking along with the bereaved. Making periodic offers of support and gestures of interest may increase the likelihood of such rare specificity on the part of the grieving.

A more corporate approach (and one that I have found to be indispensable from the standpoint of the entire community's grief process) is to have the congregation gather at the cemetery, say, on Easter morning, or Memorial Day, All Saint's Day, or at some other meaningful juncture during the church year. In such a context a service might be held, or prayers might be said, or some other symbolic gesture of remembrance might be instituted, such as the placing of flowers or the planting of a memorial tree. While those bereaved may not feel able to participate in or even attend this service (especially if their losses are recent), it still offers a kind of ministry "in absentia." For it not only recalls the reality of the loss to the church's corporate mind but reassures the bereaved that they and their lost ones are not forgotten.

I have also discovered the season of Advent (not to mention Christmas itself) to be a particularly painful period for mourners. Consequently, rather than concentrating entirely upon the joys and jubilation associated with this celebration, preachers might consider giving credence to the one great blot that appears right in the middle of Matthew's birth narrative: "The Slaughter of the Innocents." Inasmuch as the angels sing at Christ's birth, those whose lives were torn asunder by Herod's murderous rampage lift up their voices in loud lamentation. I imagine that if one were at least to inject this alternate reality into an Advent preaching or teaching series, many would resonate because of what is going on in their own hearts—a profound sense of loss, if not grief.

Cards or notes sent at peak grief times can also be tangible symbols of care. As these are sent months if not a year or more following the funeral, they serve to reinforce the notion that grief is an extended experience and to grant a sense of permission to the one grieving, expressing that in spite of society's typical denials and phobias surrounding death, it is crucial that each one of us be patient with and attentive to the process of grief.

In such written communications it would be important for you to express your availability to get together and talk (or even just to speak by phone, if that is as much closeness as the sufferer can tolerate at that point). The priority is to be intentional in your pursuit and clear about your availability.

Pastoral follow-up is a critical art too easily forgotten in a culture that would much rather sing (in the words of a popular song), "Don't worry; be happy!" Or to put it another way, "Let's avoid painful realities at all costs!" Yet, as pastoral carers seeking to show shepherdly attention to those in need, we cannot afford to allow the sheep to slip "out of sight, out of mind" during the difficult weeks and months following a tragic loss. Their welfare and wholeness depend upon our diligence and active involvement.

9

A PLEA FOR MYSTERY

It would seem that our very human need for sure, objective answers rises in proportion to the extent to which our world becomes increasingly unsure, and even unsafe. We observe the rise of religious fundamentalism worldwide, not to mention the myriad of new-found, personality-centered cults here at home, and can conclude that there is a spiritual hunger around our globe today that is reaching an almost epidemic proportion. People are willing to submit themselves to anyone and anything as long as the charismatic leader at least promises to deliver formulas, if not answers, for the world's woes. Our fears and insecurities tend to drive us to such a vulnerable position.

Suffering yields a similar kind of dynamic. The security structures sway; the foundations of stability begin to crumble; our hopes and dreams die (or worse, dissipate); and faith itself takes it "in the neck." In the throes of such an experience people languish, desperate for something concrete—for something they can stake their lives upon. And while we, as pastoral carers, are going to be tempted to supply them with just that (as if we had a quiver full of magical "answers!"), I must at this point make a plea for mystery. For theodicy is mystery; suffering is at its core mystery; God is mystery.

In a lecture given almost twenty-five years ago, John Macquarrie offers a classic treatment on the demise of mystery as a category. He begins:

> To write nowadays on mystery and, still more, to suggest that mystery has indispensable value and can provide a way to truth, is to invite the charge of being hopelessly out of touch with contemporary thought. For the history of modern science and philosophy could be interpreted as the steady elimination of mystery. Clarity and intelligibility have been the goals of that history, and there has been a truly remarkable measure of success in attaining these goals.[1]

At the close of the study Macquarrie affirms that mystery is inexhaustible and unobjectifiable, but that it is not opaque. He states that mystery possesses a translucency that not only permits us to stretch our best concepts and use them analogously but also bids us come closer, being part and parcel of what it means to be human—striving toward transcendence.[2]

The Greek term *mystery* is derived from a verb which means "to close the eyes" or "to close the mouth"[3] (the latter serving further to inform the significance of pastoral silence—see chapter 1.) It appears in the New Testament twenty-four times, mostly in the writings of Paul, who speaks of "the mysteries of God" (1 Cor. 4:1); "the mystery of God's will" (Eph. 1:9); and the mystery of Christ's presence within human beings (Col. 1:27). The remaining occurrences of the term are found in the Book of Revelation.

And while there are some who would wish to attribute the appearance of "mystery" in the New Testament wholly to the influence of the mystery cults, Raymond E. Brown concludes his study on the issue by stating:

> We believe it no exaggeration to say that, considering the variety and currency of the concept of divine mysteries in Jewish thought, Paul and the NT writers could have written everything they did about mysterion whether or not they ever encountered the pagan mystery religions. "Mystery" was a part of the native theological equipment of the Jews who came to Christ.[4]

In his classic work, *The Idea of the Holy*, Rudolf Otto speaks of our experience of the divine as *mysterium tremendum*, which involves at once the elements of awefulness, overpoweringness, urgency, wholly otherness, and fascination.[5] All of this might suggest a human posture that, though conscious of both its finitude and inability to fathom the "numinous" (divine will), is still drawn toward this One with whom we are awe-inspired. In other words, mystery, for Otto, is not only an adjunct category of our experience of the divine, but is *the* experience with the divine. It is not supplemental but integral to our first getting in touch with and then subsequently pursuing the Almighty.

The Jewish philosopher Martin Buber supplied an additional dimension to Otto's elucidation of "the Holy." Buber highlights the intimate dimensions of *mysterium tremendum* by stating:

Of course God is the "wholly Other"; but He is also the wholly Same, the wholly Present. Of course He is the Mysterium Tremendum that appears and overthrows; but He is also the mystery of the self-evident, nearer to me than my I.[6]

Buber's comments create a helpful link between the mysterious transcendence and immanence of God, a link not altogether dissimilar to Barth's conceptions of incarnation (see chapter 4). Barth felt that the reason God could indeed be the immanent one (and in his words "bear this condescension" of incarnation) was because God was also the "Almighty," capable of that which we would not ordinarily conceive nor expect.

As regards pastoral care, the concept of mystery is also indispensable. For it is not only the backdrop of our understanding of God as articulated in a theology (reminiscent of all theology being a groping "theology of pilgrims" according to Barth), but an integral dimension of persons' suffering and our approach to supporting them in that suffering. And so rather than posturing ourselves as those with ultimate answers readily at hand, I believe it would behoove all of us pastoral carers to become practiced at verbalizing the classic words, "*I don't know.*" Such a response is not only honest but categorically true. (We might practice the articulation of these words when children ask us questions that invite us to penetrate the impenetrable mysteries of life. The correct response? Make your lips form the words: "I don't know.") Not one of us knows anything about the "whys" of another person's suffering. And much to the chagrin of some, the title "Reverend" prefixed to the name of the ordained does not grant omniscient powers. We simply "do not know" when it comes to the ultimates of life.

But on the other hand, is that such a handicap? For when it all comes down to it, what is the most powerful aspect of caregiving? Inasmuch as suffering people question and rationally agonize, are they not comforted less by answers and much more by presence—divine and human? "Why me?" pales in comparison to "Thou art with me" (Psalm 23). That is what sufferers long for—companionship in their pain, not concepts, however well constructed.

With all of the seeming emphasis today upon getting down to "answers" and searching for and "claiming the promises of the Bible," I discern that there are only three foundational perspectives that we have to offer.

The first speaks of the fact that we live in a broken world. While this statement may appear to be painfully obvious on the surface, let me explore its simple yet profound ramifications. If indeed something has occurred in history that has introduced an "alien factor" into our world (see Genesis 3), then pain and tragic suffering are more the result of the environment in which we live than direct assignments from God's "Daily Planner." The "bad things" in life can then be viewed as the random effects of what has become a sick world, a world in which we have no choice but to "live and move and have our being" amidst these very painful realities. Jesus warned us about this hostile environment when he stated: "In the world you have tribulation" (John 16:33a). This is indeed our experience. Bad things happen to good people; good things happen to bad people; all kinds of things just plain happen to *all* people because we live in a broken world; we are victims of our environment.

Yet, in this same text Jesus also speaks of an ultimate overcoming: "but be of good cheer; I have overcome the world" (John 16:33b). This speaks profoundly about the basis for an ultimate, though future, hope. This hope is brought into clearer focus when Jesus also assures the disciples: "I go to prepare a place for you" (John 14:2).

This is the second perspective. It is a faith affirmation that the tribulations that we experience in this life are not the end of the story, but that an additional and rather significant chapter remains. This is a chapter, or better, a dimension that is typically termed "heaven" or "eternity"—an experience that might be compared to a journey back to the One in whom we all began.

Suffice it to say that even though this assurance that we have a destination or final "place" with God does not completely rid us of our "in the meantime" fears and woes, it certainly does inform the present. Knowing the end of the story does offer a fair degree of peace and solace in the here and now. In fact, this is precisely the destination most people think of first in our culture when faced with the prospect of death. The recent proliferation of "after-death experience" books bears testimony to the fascination—and implied concern—of so many Americans with life after death.

The third perspective comes to us in the sense of "until then, I won't leave you alone," or, to quote it more directly, "I am with you always to the end of the age" (Matt. 28:20). It speaks of the presence of God which is present to us in the spirit of Christ. God's words to Paul struggling with his mysterious "thorn in the flesh" have equal impact for persons struggling today: "My grace is sufficient for you" (2 Cor 12:9). Both expressions are assurances of Christ's abiding presence and companionship, serving further to corroborate the Psalmist's realization—"Thou art with me."

Beyond these perspectives, we have little in the way of ultimate "answers" or "promises" to offer (that is, excepting those bits of folklore and tradition—ministerial or otherwise—which serve either to set sufferers up for false expectations, or to put God "over a barrel," or both). The quoting of apocryphal adages usually ends up spelling disaster for everyone concerned.

"I don't know" is not only an accurate response from a theological/philosophical perspective but is about as honest a response as we can possibly offer a sufferer. We should become practiced at articulating these significant three words. For they represent a bona-fide embrace of the mystery that pervades all of reality and beyond.

CONCLUSION

This book does not pretend to solve the paradox of theodicy. The tension surrounding "God is great; God is good; evil is real" has existed for a long time and will most likely remain forever. What I have sought to do, however, is to preserve the place of God's omnipotence à la Karl Barth and suggest some specific ways in which it might be applied to the practice of pastoral care. Barth's rendition of power is not only more faithful to historic Christianity; its implications for the life of faith, especially when that life is battered by suffering, are most profound.

I stated earlier in this book that Rabbi Kushner's elimination of omnipotence would likely have negative effects upon three disciplines or expressions of faith: Scripture, prayer, and worship. I submit that the reframed conception of God's power as outlined within these pages not only avoids this pitfall but enhances the experience of all three disciplines.

Omnipotence in general, and this work's reinterpreted concept of omnipotence more specifically, is faithful to the Scriptures of the Old and New Testaments. It is consistent with what has been revealed there about God. Those who choose to move beyond biblical bounds must have good reasons for so doing, assuming that a book that has historically occupied such a high place in the life and faith of the church will continue so to do.

Second, I would submit that prayer is brought alive by this redefinition and reaffirmation of God's power. For now God expresses God's power through identification and empathy. God's power is personal, not aloof; proximate, not removed. Thus it is made more accessible through this reinterpretation which not only casts a new light upon the purpose of that power (intimate identification) but also pinpoints the very channels through which God chooses to work: alienation, weakness, vulnerability, pain, suffering. Such a God is able to hear and identify with my prayers and groans. There is much power for prayer in this vision of God's ultimate empathy.

Finally, a God who possesses the kind of omnipotence that is able to "bend down" in love truly transcends all humanly devised attributes. This power is not proud. It can bear the extravagance of humble and empathic love. I not only desire to worship such a God, I cannot help but worship such a God. For I am wooed by such a wondrous love as this. This is a powerful love that spares no expense. Through Christ it goes to the point of suffering with and for us as objects of that pursuing love. All that I can do is be lost in wonder, love, and praise. In this sense worship, too, is enhanced by an omnipotence redefined.

These are the ways in which the power of God might now be envisioned and applied to the life of faith. It is especially cogent for those for whom this book is mostly directed—those who tragically suffer and those who minister to sufferers.

Suffering will not disappear from this world until the One in whom it all began returns again to bring it to an end. In the meantime evil and nothingness will continue to bring about "bad things," thereby causing all of those who ask "Why?" great distress and quandary.

Yet the greatest quandary when it comes to "bad things happening to good people" is not ours but God's, according to Douglas John Hall. It is God who is faced with the quandry of love.

> What I mean, to put it in the most childish way, is that God's problem is not that God *is not able* to do certain things. God's problem is that God loves! Love complicates the life of God as it complicates every life. . . . If God is to "get at" the greatest sources of human misery (which is certainly related to sin in the biblical perspective), God *must* (being love!) enter upon a plan or "economy" more complex and indirect than the "simple" meting out of justice. As I have expressed this economy here, it involves an approach which is not only complex but costly; for it means that God's *power* has ultimately to articulate itself in divine solidarity with the sufferer, that is, in the "weakness" of suffering love.[1]

This summarizes well what I would substitute for Rabbi Kushner's no-longer-omnipotent God. For I can think of nothing more powerful or significant to both a victim of tragic suffering and a pastoral carer than a God who, through the omnipotence of suffering love, "suffers with."

NOTES

INTRODUCTION

1. J. Christiaan Beker, *Suffering and Hope* (Philadelphia: Fortress Press, 1987), 83.

1. BEFORE YOU ENTER

1. Thomas C. Oden, *Care of Souls in the Classic Tradition* (Philadelphia: Fortress Press, 1984), 18.

2. Ibid.

3. Ibid.

4. Carlyle Marney, *Priests to Each Other* (Valley Forge: Judson Press, 1974), 29.

5. Paul Pruyser, *The Minister as Diagnostician* (Philadelphia: Westminster Press, 1976), 47–48.

6. I am not sure what the female counterpart would be.

7. Martin Buber, *I and Thou*, trans. R. G. Smith, 2d ed. (New York: Scribner, 1958), 78.

8. Frederick Buechner, *Telling the Truth* (San Francisco: Harper & Row, 1977), 16.

9. Walter Wangerin, *Ragman and Other Cries of Faith*, (San Francisco: Harper & Row, 1984), 62.

2. ASSESSING WHAT SUFFERERS SEEK

1. The term strictly means to interrupt the flow of a musical piece. See note under "Music" in the *Interpreter's Dictionary of the Bible*, vol. 3 (Nashville: Abingdon, 1966), 460.

2. See Granger E. Westberg, *Good Grief* (Philadelphia: Fortress Press, 1971).

4. THEODICY: THE PROBLEM OF EVIL

1. William Hendricks, *A Theology for Children* (Nashville: Broadman Press, 1980), 143.

2. Psalms 10, 13, 25, 35, 42; 2 Cor. 12:7-10.

3. See John Hick, *Evil and the God of Love*, 2d ed. (London: Macmillan, 1977), for an excellent historical study of theodicy.

4. Edwin Franden Dakin, *Mrs. Eddy: The Biography of a Virginal Mind* (New York: Charles Scribner's Sons, 1930), 102.

5. Mary Baker Eddy, *Science and Health with Key to the Scriptures* (Boston: Trustees under the Will of Mary Baker G. Eddy, 1875), 107–64.

6. The ancient Zoroastrians are an additional example; however, their brand of dualism did give God a slight edge over evil and the devil.

7. Harold Kushner, *When Bad Things Happen to Good People* (New York: Avon Books, 1981), 42–43.

8. Ibid., 45.

9. J. Christiaan Beker, *Suffering and Hope* (Philadelphia: Fortress Press) 83–84.

10. Douglas John Hall, *God and Human Suffering* (Minneapolis: Augsburg, 1986), 153.

11. Ibid., 154.

12. Genesis 1–2; Exodus 3–4; Deuteronomy 1; Job 40–42; Pss. 8, 18, 19, 29, 46, 93, 148; Isaiah 6; Mark 9:1; Luke 1:35; Rom. 1:20; 1 Cor. 1:18; Rev. 7:12;19:1.

13. Hall, *God and Human Suffering*, 152.

14. Matt. 6:9-14, and footnote (RSV) New Testament Section 2d ed., © 1971.

15. Franklin M. Segler, *Christian Worship: Its Theology and Practice* (Nashville: Broadman Press, 1967), 5.

16. See Rudolph Otto, *The Idea of the Holy*, trans. John Harvey (New York: Oxford University Press, 1950).

17. Kushner, *When Bad Things Happen to Good People*, 136.

18. Ibid., 139.

19. Hall, *God and Human Suffering*, 155. See also Jürgen Moltmann, *Jesus Christ for Today's World* (Minneapolis: Fortress Press, 1994), who directs us to the suffering God of the Cross.

5. KARL BARTH SPEAKS OUT ON EVIL

1. Gregory G. Bolich, *Karl Barth and Evangelicalism* (Downers Grove, Ill.: InterVarsity Press, 1980), 117.

2. Karl Barth, *Church Dogmatics* IV/1, §14, ed. G. W. Bromiley and T. F. Torrance (Edinburgh: T&T Clark, 1936–1969), 186.

3. Ibid., 176.

4. 2 Cor. 5:19.

5. Barth, *Church Dogmatics* IV/1, §14: 176.

6. Ibid., 177.

7. Ibid., 176.

8. Ibid., 159.

9. Luke 15:11-32.

10. Matt. 3:17.

11. Barth, *Church* Dogmatics IV/1, §14: 158.

12. Ibid., 159.

13. *Church Dogmatics* III/3, §11: 365.

14. Ibid., 289.

15. Ibid., 349.

16. See note under this Latin term in Richard A. Muller, *Dictionary of Latin and Greek Theological Terms* (Grand Rapids: Baker, 1985).

17. Barth, *Church Dogmatics* III/3, §11: 293.

18. Ibid., 351.

19. Ibid., 352.

20. John Hick, *Evil and the Love of God*, 2d ed. (London: Macmillan, 1977) 135.

21. Barth, *Church Dogmatics* III/3, §11: 367.

22. Ibid.

23. Ibid.

6. PASTORAL CARE: WHERE THEOLOGY TOUCHES DOWN

1. 2 Cor. 12:9.

2. Douglas John Hall, *God and Human Suffering* (Minneapolis: Augsburg, 1986), 158.

3. Thomas C. Oden, *Care of Souls in the Classic Tradition* (Philadelphia: Fortress Press, 1984), 19.

4. Ibid., 18.

5. Arthur C. McGill, *Suffering: A Test of Theological Method* (Philadelphia: Westminster Press, 1968), 85.

6. Oden, *Care of Souls*, 26.

7. Karl Barth, *Church Dogmatics* III, ed. G. W. Bromiley and T. F. Torrance (Edinburgh: T&T Clark, 1936–1969), 367.

8. 1 Thess. 4:13.

9. J. Christiaan Beker, *Suffering and Hope* (Philadelphia: Fortress Press) 73.

10. 1 Cor. 15:54.

11. Rom. 8:35-39.

12. Barth, *Church Dogmatics* III, 367.

13. Hall, *God and Human Suffering*, 197.

8. NOW THE FUNERAL'S OVER

1. See Glen C. Davidson, *Understanding Mourning* (Minneapolis: Augsburg, 1984), 49f.

2. Ibid, 68.

9. A PLEA FOR MYSTERY

1. John Macquarrie, *Mystery and Truth* (Milwaukee: Marquette University Theology Department, 1973), 55.

2. Ibid., 93–95.

3. Ibid., 69.

4. Raymond E. Brown, *The Semitic Background on the Term "Mystery" in the New Testament* (Philadelphia: Fortress Press, 1968), 69.

5. Rudolph Otto, *The Idea of the Holy*, trans. John Harvey (New York: Oxford University Press, 1950), 12f.

6. Martin Buber, *I and Thou*, trans. R. G. Smith, 2d ed. (New York: Charles Scribner's Sons, 1958), 79.

CONCLUSION

1. Douglas John Hall, *God and Human Suffering* (Minneapolis: Augsburg, 1986), 156. See also William Placher, *Narratives of a Vulnerable God* (Louisville: Westminster/John Knox Press, 1994), who also keys on the vulnerability of God.

SELECTED
BIBLIOGRAPHY

Beker, J. Christiaan. *Suffering and Hope: The Biblical Vision and the Human Predicament.* Philadelphia: Fortress, 1987.

Buechner, Frederick. *Telling the Truth.* New York: Harper & Row, 1977.

Davidson, Glen W. *Understanding Mourning.* Minneapolis: Augsburg, 1984.

Drakeford, John. *People To People Therapy.* New York: Harper & Row, 1978.

Hall, Douglas John. *God and Human Suffering: An Exercise in the Theology of the Cross.* Minneapolis: Augsburg, 1986.

Hick, John. *Evil and the God of Love.* New York: Harper & Row, 1966.

Mace, Nancy L., and Peter V. Rabins. *The 36-Hour Day.* New York: Warner, 1981.

May, Gerald. *Addiction and Grace.* New York: Harper & Row, 1988.

Mitford, Jessica. *The American Way of Death.* New York: Fawcett, 1963.

Moltmann, Jürgen. *Jesus Christ for Today's World.* Minneapolis: Fortress Press, 1994.

Nouwen, Henri J. M. *In the Name of Jesus*. New York: Crossroad, 1995.

———. *The Wounded Healer*. New York: Doubleday, Image Books, 1972.

Oates, Wayne. *The Religious Care of the Psychiatric Patient*. Philadelphia: Westminister, 1978.

Oden, Thomas. *Care of the Souls in the Classic Tradition*. Philadelphia: Fortress Press, 1984.

———. *Kerygma and Counseling*. Philadelphia: Westminister, 1966.

———. *Pastoral Counsel*. New York: Crossroad, 1989.

Placher, William C. *Narratives of a Vulnerable God*. Louisville: Westminister John Knox, 1994.

Pruyser, Paul. *The Minister as Diagnostician*. Philadelphia: Westminister, 1976.

Stone, Howard. *Crisis Counseling*. Revised Edition. Creative Pastoral and Counseling. Minneapolis: Fortress Press, 1993.

———. *The Word of God and Pastoral Care*. Nashville: Abingdon, 1988.

Westberg, Granger E. *Good Grief*. Minneapolis: Fortress Press, 1971.